First World War
and Army of Occupation
War Diary
France, Belgium and Germany

58 DIVISION
175 Infantry Brigade
London Regiment
9th (County of London) Battalion (Queen Victoria's Rifles)
1 February 1918 - 16 February 1919

WO95/3009/1

The Naval & Military Press Ltd
www.nmarchive.com
Published in association with The National Archives

Published by

The Naval & Military Press Ltd

Unit 10 Ridgewood Industrial Park,

Uckfield, East Sussex,

TN22 5QE England

Tel: +44 (0) 1825 749494

www.naval-military-press.com

www.nmarchive.com

This diary has been reprinted in facsimile from the original. Any imperfections are inevitably reproduced and the quality may fall short of modern type and cartographic standards.

© **Crown Copyright**
Images reproduced by permission of The National Archives, London, England, 2015.

Contents

Document type	Place/Title	Date From	Date To
Heading	WO95/3009/1 1/9 Battalion London Reg Queen Victoria's Rifles.		
Heading	58 Division 175 Brigade 1/9 London Regt 1918 Feb-1919 Feb From 56 Div 169 Bde To 2 Div 2 Light Bn		
Heading	War Diary Of 9th Battalion London Regiment Period From 1st February 1918 To 28th February 1918 Volume 13		
War Diary	La Neuville	01/02/1918	07/02/1918
War Diary	Marest	08/02/1918	08/02/1918
War Diary	Riez Camp	09/02/1918	09/02/1918
War Diary	Liez Quarry	10/02/1918	21/02/1918
War Diary	Rouez Camp	25/02/1918	25/02/1918
War Diary	Les Buttes De Rouy	26/02/1918	28/02/1918
Heading	War Diary (Volume III) 9th London Regt (Q V R) March 1918		
War Diary	Amigny Rouy	01/03/1918	10/03/1918
War Diary	Buttes De Rouy	18/03/1918	30/03/1918
Heading	175th Inf. Bde. 58th Div. War Diary 9th Battn. The London Regiment. (Queen Victoria's Rifles). April 1918.		
Heading	War Diary 9 London Regt. QVR Volume IV. April 1918.		
War Diary	Pierremande	02/04/1918	02/04/1918
War Diary	Praast	03/04/1918	03/04/1918
War Diary	Le Mesnil	04/04/1918	04/04/1918
War Diary	Coutry	05/04/1918	09/04/1918
War Diary	Villers Brettoneux	09/04/1918	12/04/1918
War Diary	Boves	13/04/1918	15/04/1918
War Diary	Blangy	15/04/1918	26/04/1918
War Diary	Pont De Metz	27/04/1918	27/04/1918
War Diary	Riencourt	28/04/1918	28/04/1918
War Diary	Ailly	29/04/1918	30/04/1918
Heading	War Diary 9th London Regt (QVR) Volume V May 1918.		
War Diary	Ailly-Le-Haut-Clocher	01/05/1918	05/05/1918
War Diary	Bois Robert	06/05/1918	06/05/1918
War Diary	Baizieux	07/05/1918	31/05/1918
Heading	9th Battn. London Regiment (Queen Victoria's Rifles) War Diary From 1st June 1918 To 30th June 1918. Vol 17.		
War Diary	C.20.b	01/06/1918	04/06/1918
War Diary	B.9.d.1.4. S.E. of Molliens Au Bois.	05/06/1918	16/06/1918
War Diary	Bougainville	17/06/1918	17/06/1918
War Diary	Molliens Au Bois	18/06/1918	18/06/1918
War Diary	Baizieux	19/06/1918	30/06/1918
Map			
Map	Map A		
Heading	War Diary Volume VII 1st July 1918 To 31st July 9th Bn London Regt QVR		
War Diary	Ref. 1/40000 62D	01/07/1918	01/07/1918

War Diary	D.11.C. D.23.a.D.17.b.	01/07/1918	25/07/1918
War Diary	C.6.c.3.3	26/07/1918	31/07/1918
Map			
Map	Angres		
Map	Map D		
Heading	175th Bde. 58th Div. 9th Battalion London Regiment (Queen Victoria Rifles). August 1918.		
Heading	War Diary Of 9th Battalion London Regiment (Queen Victorias Rifles). From 1st August 1918 To 31st August 1918. Vol 19.		
War Diary	Darwin Reserve Trench D.17.23	01/08/1918	03/08/1918
War Diary	Vignacourt	04/08/1918	06/08/1918
War Diary	Bois Escardonneuse	07/08/1918	07/08/1918
War Diary	Mallar Wood	09/08/1918	09/08/1918
War Diary	Bois De Tailles	10/08/1918	12/08/1918
War Diary	Bois Escardonneuse	13/08/1918	31/08/1918
Heading	War Diary 9th London Regt. September 1918.		
Heading	32nd Division Pioneers M.G.C. September 1918.		
Heading	War Diary of 9th Battn. London Regiment (Queen Victoria's Rifles) From 1st September 1918 To 30th September 1918 (Volume 1)		
War Diary	Farny Mill	01/09/1918	30/09/1918
Heading	Q.V.R. (9/London Regt). Copy of personal notes on operations from August 12th. 1918. to September 26th. 1918. From Major W.H. Lindsay-Renton, DSO., TD.,		
Miscellaneous	Notes on Operations etc of Q.V.R. between August 12th and September. 26th.		
Heading	Q.V.R. (9/London Regt). Copy Of personal notes on operations from August 12th. 1918. to September 26th. 1918. From Major W.H. Lindsay-Renton, DSO., TD.,		
Miscellaneous	Notes on Operations Etc Of Q.V.R. Between August 12th and September. 26th.		
War Diary		01/10/1918	31/10/1918
Heading	War Diary of 9th Battn London Regiment (Queen Victoria's Rifles) From 1st November 1918 To 30th November 1918. Vol 22.		
War Diary	Rumegies	01/11/1918	10/11/1918
War Diary	Ecacharies	11/11/1918	12/11/1918
War Diary	Stambruges.	13/11/1918	30/11/1918
Heading	War Diary of 9th Battn London Regt. (Queen Victoria's Rifles) Period 1st December To 31st December 1918. Vol 23.		
War Diary	Stambruges	01/12/1918	19/12/1918
War Diary	Leuze	20/12/1918	31/12/1918
Heading	War Diary Of 9th Battn London Regiment (Queen Victorias Rifles) Period From 1st January 1919 To 31st January 1919. Vol 24.		
War Diary	Leuze	01/01/1919	28/02/1919
War Diary	Leuze	01/02/1919	16/02/1919

WO95
3009/1

1/9 Battalion London Regt
Queen Victoria's
Rifles.

58 DIVISION

175 BRIGADE

1/9 LONDON REGT

1918 FEB - 1919 FEB

FROM 56 DIV 169 BDE

TO 2 DIV 24(?) BR(?)

(1/9 BN ABSORBED 2/9 BN 1918 FEB)

Confidential

War Diary
— of —
9th Battalion London Regiment
(Queen Victoria's Rifles)

Period from 1st February 1918 to 28th February 1918

Volume

WAR DIARY or INTELLIGENCE SUMMARY

Army Form C. 2118.

Place	Date	Hour	Summary of Events and Information	Remarks and references to Appendices
LA NEUVILLE	1/9/18		Battalion Parade & Re-inorganisation of Nos 1,2,3,4 + 2nd Battalion Head. forward	
"	2/9/18		Nr. Brown was to the 9/c London Regt	
"			Battalion Parade for drill order to be conducted by platoon training & classes to meet	
"	3/9/18		Voluntary Church Service	
"	4/9/18		Battalion Parade followed by platoon training	
"	5/9/18		" "	
"	6/9/18		" "	
"	7/9/18		The Battalion entrained at CORBIE (I.34.C.4) for ATILLY (M.23 A 3.3) & proceeded by route march to MAREST (L.8.a.1.8) Having billeted there for the night	Sheet 62D & 70E
MAREST	8/9/18		The Battalion marched to ROUEZ (S.24.d.3.2.) C & D Coys proceeding to LIEZ FORT (N.34.c.4.3) relieving the 12/London Regt	Sheet 66 SW
RIEZ CAMP	9/9/18		Battalion H.Q. & B Coy proceeded to billets at LIEZ (N.32.c.5.4) A Coy proceeded the relief at MENNESSIS (M.36.d.5.0)	
LIEZ QUARRY	10/9/18		Selecting dispositions of posts by Coy Commanders on the lollois ground about in the intended commencement of FORT LIEZ & improvement to Nillets	

T2134. Wt. W708-776. 500000. 4/15. Sir J. C. & S.

WAR DIARY or INTELLIGENCE SUMMARY.

Army Form C. 2118.

(Erase heading not required.)

Place	Date	Hour	Summary of Events and Information	Remarks and references to Appendices
LIEZ QUARRY	11/9/18		Working part & taking Inspection of post in the Battle Zone around FORT LIEZ. Inspection of post by commanding officer.	
"	12/9/18		C & D Coys working on improvement of communication of FORT LIEZ. A Coy working under R.E. instructions on their line of defence. B Coy having orders to garrison internet	
"	13/9/18		Coys working on their lines of defence, & improvements to FORT LIEZ	
"	14/9/18		" " " " "	
"	15/9/18 to the 22/9/18		Coys working on their posts in the Battle Zone around FORT LIEZ area	
"	24/9/18		The Battalion was relieved in the line by the 7th Battn London, & proceeded to ROVEZ Sheet No. 66c S.W.	Sheet No. 66c S.W.
"			CAMP (S.24 central) by route march, where it was billeted for the night	No. 70 D N.W.
RIVEZ CAMP	25/9/18		The Battalion proceeded by movement to LES BUTTES DE ROUY (H.1.c.6.3.) relieving the 6th Battn London Regt in the Battle Zone. A & B Coys being billeted at SINCENY (G.10.6.2.2.) in support	No. 70 D N.W.
LES BUTTES DE ROUY	26/9/18		Last Surrey Regt in the Battle Zone. A & B Coys being in the line the front being from (B.23.a.3.2.) the shelf (H.5.a.5.2.) C Coy on the right D Coy on the right A & B Coys in support	No. 70 D N.W.
"	27/9/18 & 28/9/18		Battalion holding the line	

Mitchell
Capt. & Adjt.
18th Battn London Regt.
(Cost. London Irish)

WAR DIARY
or
INTELLIGENCE SUMMARY

Army Form C. 2118.

Place	Date	Hour	Summary of Events and Information	Remarks and references to Appendices
AMIGNY ROUY	1/3/18		The 10th R.I.R. Battalion Holding the front line from B.23.a.53 to H.5c.29 turning thus (Sketch Map D.N.W.)	
			The mud & wire caused much work to improve particular dispositions	
			Battalion H.Q. were at Mon Bichon at (B.24.d.75.48) Two Coys in R Quarters	76th NW
			where in the support line approx between B.24.b.72 & H.3.C.47	
			The Battalion was relieved by the 10th Lanc^s Reg^t & moved back to the Buttes	
	10/3/18		Scene in L BUTTES DE ROUY were. Battalion H.Q., the Lewis gun school (Rangers) in the Keep	70^D NW
BUTTES DE ROUY	13/3/18		Battalion relieved the 10th Lancs Reg^t & the Coys of the Rangers & Battalion H.Q. at H.1a.9.1	
			Line Four Coys from B.23.a.53 to H.5c.29 Battalion H.Q. at H.3.a.61	"
			Order of Coys from right to left W.B.C.D.A.	
	19/3/18		B & C Coys relieved by Coys of the Rangers & moved into support B & C Coys at B.24.d.9.8 & C.C. & V.B.D.C. Battalion H.Q. remained (B.24.d.75.48)	
	20/3/16		9 PM orders to be in support for attack come through & all troops were manned	
	21/3/18	4 AM	on a frontage of Montescourt - AMIGNY ROUY Heavy shell on attack did not come up to expectation	(H.I.K.B.24.)
			on the morning of 24/25/3/18 Battalion was in Reserve to the supported divs	
AMIGNY ROUY, BILLE			evening of AMIGNY ROUY Battalion H.Q. at L. BUTTES DE ROUY	
night of	29/30 - 1/3/18		Battalion relieved from the line by the 10th Lewisham Regt & moved back to the	

WAR DIARY
or
INTELLIGENCE SUMMARY.

(Erase heading not required.)

Army Form C. 2118.

Place	Date	Hour	Summary of Events and Information	Remarks and references to Appendices
			Intermediate line running along the bank of the River OISER and East of BICHANCOURT (G.20.C) facing North	70 DNN

Signed,
O.C. 5th Battn. London Regt.
(Queen Victoria's Rifles.)

175th Inf.Bde.
58th Div.

9th BATTN. THE LONDON REGIMENT.
(QUEEN VICTORIA'S RIFLES).

A P R I L

1 9 1 8

Jul 15

175/58

Army Form C. 2118.

WAR DIARY
or
INTELLIGENCE SUMMARY.
(Erase heading not required.)

Instructions regarding War Diaries and Intelligence Summaries are contained in F. S. Regs., Part II. and the Staff Manual respectively. Title pages will be prepared in manuscript.

Place	Date	Hour	Summary of Events and Information	Remarks and references to Appendices
PIERREMANDE	2/4/18		The Battalion was relieved by the French 363rd Regt. & marched to PRAAST (M3C45) where it was billeted for the night	Sheet N° Sketch 4/D
PRAAST	3/4/18		The Battalion proceeded by route march to LE MESNIL (B19 d16) reaching there the same night	4/D
LE MESNIL	4/4/18		Proceeded to COUTRY by route march	
COUTRY	5/4/18		Proceeded to VILLERS COTTEREUX by route march & from entrained for LONGEAU (M9R4) arriving at 11.30 p.m. & marched to Hout aux BOYES (M17c04) where the Battalion rested	62/D
	6/4/15		In the afternoon the Battalion took over a holding a line from (N16A)4 (T12b83) Batt H.Q. on the hill at (T11C83)	62 D
	7/4/18		At dawn the Battalion moved up to the French line in support of French Cav.	
			VILLERS BRETTONEUX (Q.35) alternary B. Gun took Batt: H.Q. at (Q.35c19) in the hill & lay in support Batt. ABDEp.	62/D
			The Battalion relieved on the line by the 10th Lancs. Regt. & moved back to	
VILLERS BRETTONEUX	9/4/18		Villers BOYES (T.T)	62/D
	10/4/18 & 12/4/18		Battalion at BOYES rested	

Army Form C. 2118.

WAR DIARY
or
INTELLIGENCE SUMMARY.
(Erase heading not required.)

Instructions regarding War Diaries and Intelligence Summaries are contained in F. S. Regs., Part II. and the Staff Manual respectively. Title pages will be prepared in manuscript.

Place	Date	Hour	Summary of Events and Information	Remarks and references to Appendices
BOVES	13/4/18		The Battalion moved up to the Reserve line running from (F.30.d.) (V.19.a.5.5) to BOIS DE GENTELLES (T.11.c.9.5) (T.30.a.) Battalion Batt. H.Q. at BOIS DE GENTELLES (T.11.c.9.5.)	62D
	13/4/18		Battalion relieved by the 38th Australian Batt'y. and moved back to new billets at BLANGY (N.82 central)	62D
BLANGY			Battalion relieved the 3rd London Regt. on the Reserve line running from (U.13.c.8.0) to (T.30.d.5.0.) Batt. H.Q. at (T.11.c.8.2.)	"
	24/4/18	3.45 a.m.	At 3.45 a.m. the Bosche opened up a very heavy bombardment in BOIS DE HANGARD. H.Q. moved to (U.19.a.2.3) at 8 a.m. Bosche attacked at 9 p.m. Battalions moved up to (V.7.b.7.) a.s.c.h. and were in position for counter-attack. At 8.30 p.m. Batt. moved to relieve front line running from (U.6.b.8.4) along edge of wood of Bois to (U.22.b.5.3.) 'A' 'B' & 'C' Coys attacked only occupying known D Coy were unable to form up in the open. The H.Q. Company in support of them in line running from (U.6.b.0.5) to (U.21.b.1.5) moved to point of 'C' Coys front. Few casualties, however it was impossible to establish limit of 'A' 'B' & 'C' Coys on the left, the Battalion on the left of Battalion to confirm and the situation remaining at its extreme left unknown. 65 Prisoners. 8 M.G. Material. 6 cars were captured and 65 prisoners.	60D

WAR DIARY

PLACE	DATE		
	25/4/18	In the evening the Battalion was relieved in the line by the 8th Queens & moved back to a camp in a wood at (N31b)	62D
	26/4/18	The Battalion proceeded by route march to billets at PONT DE METZ (2.C.5.7.)	AMIENS. 1/100000
PONT DE METZ	27/4/18	" " " at RIENCOURT (1.A.5.2.)	"
RIENCOURT	28/4/18	The Battalion marched to billets at AILLY LE HAUT CLOCHER (6.L.9.6.)	ABBEVILLE 1/100000
AILLY	29 & 30	Battalion resting	

[signature]

WAR DIARY
or
INTELLIGENCE SUMMARY.

(Erase heading not required.)

Army Form C. 2118.

War Diary
9th London Regt
(Q.V.R)

Volume V May 1916

WAR DIARY or INTELLIGENCE SUMMARY

Army Form C. 2118.

Place	Date	Hour	Summary of Events and Information	Remarks and references to Appendices
AILLY-LE-HAUT-CLOCHER	May 1st May 2 - 3 - 4 - 5		Battalion in rest billets. " " " 	ABBEVILLE. 1/100,000.
BOIS ROBERT	May 6		Battalion Battle Surplus proceeded to VILLERS-SOUS-AILLY. 58(London) Division moved into 3rd Corps Reserve. Battalion left AILLY-LE-HAUT-CLOCHER in busses at 10.0 p.m. and debussed at CONTAY. Battalion marched to BOIS ROBERT at C11.6/15.05 and remained there in bivouac for the night.	62 D. 1/20.000. 57 D 1/20.000
BAIZIEUX	May 7		Battalion moved forward to the BAIZIEUX Defence System with Bn. H.Q. at C6d 75.35. Line running D7 central to V29 central. A Company relieved one company of ROYAL WEST KENTS. C Company relieved 19th Bn. London Regt. B and D moved into hitherto unoccupied trenches.	
	May 8		B. C. and D Companies moved forward to line running from BAIZIEUX Defence Line at D1 d 0.2. running N.E. & SE. to V25 d 5.4. A Company remained in tent position. Battalion worked under the R.E. on the BAIZIEUX Defence Line. Found areas reconnoitred.	
	May 9 May 15 May 16		175 Inf. Brigade relieved 141 Inf. Brigade 47 (London) Division in the left sub-sector running W21 a 5.9. to W26 G 0.0. The Bn. relieved the 19th Bn. the London Regt. W21 c 5.7. to W27 a 2.6. with Bn. H.Q. at W25 c 2.8. B and D Coy's in the front line. A in support. C in Reserve. BAIZIEUX Defence Line taken over by 23rd Bn. London Regt.	
	May 17 May 18		Quiet day on battalion front. British Artillery active. Battle Artillery active in the evening. Working party of 50 had 19 casualties owing to enemy an enfiladed shoot about W27 a 0.2.8 at 11.30 p.m.	
	May 19		Enemy Trench Mortars on front line at 1-1.15am. Considerable shelling of support and reserve trenches. Heavy shelling over whole Bn. area from 10.30pm to 11.30pm.	R. J. Lindsay Parker Major Commanding Queen Victoria's Rifles.

WAR DIARY
or
INTELLIGENCE SUMMARY
(Erase heading not required.)

Army Form C. 2118.

Place	Date	Hour	Summary of Events and Information	Remarks and references to Appendices
	May 20		Heavy bombardment of front line at 3:30 a.m. 2/Lieut. E.F. DICKINS wounded. Battalion relieved by 12th Bn. 1st LONDON Regt: the RANGERS and moved back into Brigade Reserve. Bn. H.Q. and C Company in the MAZE. A and B Company in MURRAY TRENCH from V.24.c.9.9. to V.24.d.6.5.0.0. D Company in MELBOURNE TRENCH W.19.b.7.4.	
	May 21		Working Parties under the R.E. Bn. H.Q. shelled with gas shells about 11pm.	
	May 22		Gas shelling of Bn. H.Q. and MURRAY TRENCH at 2 a.m. and 9.30 p.m. Bn. H.Q. shelled with H.E. at 3.30 p.m. Seven Runners wounded. Brigade relieved by 173 Inf. Brigade. Bn. relieved by 3/4 Bn. LONDON Regt. moving into COURT SYSTEM of trenches (V.22 and V.23) vacated by 2/2 Bn. LONDON Regt. Bn. H.Q. in V.22.b.45.70 under the bank on the HENENCOURT – SENLIS Road.	
	May 23 May 24		Bn. in COURT System of trenches. Battle order plans changed over.	
	May 25		Reconnaissance of right sub-sector carried out.	
	May 26		Bn. worked on COURT and POSSUM TRENCH V.23.b.	
	May 27		173 Inf. Brigade relieved 174 Inf. Brigade in right centre sector of 58th Divl. Front. Bn. relieved the 7th Bn. LONDON Regt. in the night from W.2.G.4.5. to A.C.35.9.5. C Company in right. A on left, D in support and B in Reserve. Bn. H.Q. MURRAY TRENCH V.30.b.4.5.	
	May 28		Quiet day on Bn. front.	
	May 29		Quiet day on Bn. front.	
	May 30		Hostile Artillery more active in the evening on the MAZE at V.24 d.2.2. Considerable enemy gas shelling from 2.30 a.m. to 3.30 a.m. turned the MAZE and Bn. H.Q. R.M. Lindsay – Ranks	
	May 31		Major Commanding Queen Victoria's Rifles	

Vol 17

Confidential

9th Battn. London Regiment
(Queen Victoria's Rifles)

War Diary

From 1st June 1918 to 30th June 1918.

Army Form C. 2118.

WAR DIARY
or
INTELLIGENCE SUMMARY.
(Erase heading not required.)

Place	Date	Hour	Summary of Events and Information	Remarks and references to Appendices
Ezob.	1.		First day out of the trenches. Battalion cleaning up.	6 2 D. 1/140,000
	2.		Church Parade. Service in the wood.	
	3.		Company Training.	
	4.		Battalion dug a cable line East of WARLOY.	
Bq 91.4. S.E. of MOLLIENS AU BOIS.	5.		Brigade moved to a wood S.E. of MOLLIENS – AU – BOIS. Route BEHENCOURT – MONTIGNY. Bn. H.Q. established at Bq 91.4.	
	6.			
	7.		Bn. Training and Specialist Courses.	
	8.			
	9.		Church Parade at Bq 95.65. Annual Gas Demonstration.	
	10.		Warning Order for a move received at 2.30 a.m. 58 Division handed over from III Corps to XXII Corps. Brigade marched to VILLERS – BOCAGE and entrained. Debussed at BRIDOEMERNIL. Battalion marched to BOUGAINVILLE to tent billets vacated by 37th Division.	ANIENS 1/100,000.
	11.			
	12.			
	13.		Battalion training.	
	14.			
	15.			
	16.		Battalion won Brigade Lewis Gun Competition. Church Parade.	

Lieut. Col. Cunningham,
Queen Victoria Rifles.

WAR DIARY
or
INTELLIGENCE SUMMARY.

Army Form C. 2118.

Place	Date	Hour	Summary of Events and Information	Remarks and references to Appendices
BOUGAINVILLE	17.		Battalion training.	
MOLLIENS AU BOIS	18		58 Division taken over Corps. Bayonet moved by bus via AMIENS (by-passed) in Bde P.E. of MOLLIENS AU BOIS. Battle Surplus proceeded to MIRVAUX. Bn. took over camp vacated by 2/2 Londons.	62.B
BAIZIEUX	19		175 Inf. Bayonet relieved 173 Inf. Bayonet in Divisional Reserve the Bn. relieved 3rd London Regt. in BAIZIEUX System from 016.45.2.0. to B7.C.9.1. Bn. H.Q. C6c 3.3.	
	20.		BAIZIEUX Line.	
	21.		The Battalion worked on LAVIEVILLE Support line at night.	
	22		The Battalion worked in LAVIEVILLE Support line at night.	
	23.		Right half sector of Bn. front reconnoitred from E13c 65.80 to E19 6 0.5.	
	24.		175 Inf. Bayonet relieved the 174 Inf. Bde. on the night. The Battalion relieved the 6 London Regt. in the right sub-sector (E13c 65.80 to E19 6 0.5.) D Coy. sustained casualties on the way up to the line.	
	25.		Quiet Day. D Coy. sustained casualties from enemy trench mortars.	
	26.		Quiet Day.	
	27.			
	28.		The Bn. relieved by 12 London Regt. and moved into Support in DIAMOND TRENCH, DARWIN Reserve and DARLING Reserve.	
	29.		Quiet Day.	
	30.			

Lieut-Colonel Commdg.
Queen Victoria's Rifles.

MAP A.

Army Form C. 2118.

WAR DIARY
or
INTELLIGENCE SUMMARY.
(Erase heading not required.)

WD/18

War Diary

Volume VII

1st July 1918 to 31st July 1918

9th B. London Regt

QVR

WAR DIARY
or
INTELLIGENCE SUMMARY

Army Form C. 2118.

9th Bn. London Regt. Queen Victoria's Rifles

Place	Date	Hour	Summary of Events and Information	Remarks and references to Appendices
Rd. 74.0000.62D	1918 JULY			
D.11.C. D.23.a.	1		Battalion in Support & Right Sector. Battle Surplus changed over.	
D.14.b.	2		Quiet day except from 9.30–10.30 p.m. when enemy trench mortars attacked on left of Bn. front. Battalion relieved 10th Bn. London Regt. in Left Sub Sector, front line.	
	3		Fairly quiet day.	
	4		Coys on right attacked enemy position. Bn. front bombarded by enemy, causing casualties. 4 Killed. 10 Wounded.	
	5		Quiet day. Gas projectors fired from Bn. front. No enemy retaliation.	
	6		Battalion relieved in the line by 2/4th Londons & moved into LAVIEVILLE-BAIZIEUX Sector.	
	7		Moved by 2/2nd Londons. Cleaning up & Baths.	
	8		8.30 p.m. Orders received to man Battle Positions. All companies in position by 11.25 p.m.	
	9		2 Companies in LAVIEVILLE Sector exchanged with 2 Companies in BAIZIEUX Sector.	
	10		Cleaning up & Baths. Working parties under R.E.	
	11			
	12		Battalion relieved by 4th Londons in Right Sub Sector of Left Sector.	
	13		Quiet day. Hostile barrage at midnight 13/14th. No casualties.	
	14		Fairly quiet day. Battle Surplus exchanged.	
	15		Hostile artillery above normal. 3 O.Rks. Killed. 1 Off. 1 O.Rk. Wounded.	

WAR DIARY
or
INTELLIGENCE SUMMARY.

Army Form C. 2118.

Place	Date	Hour	Summary of Events and Information	Remarks and references to Appendices
	1918 JULY 16		Fairly quiet day. Enemy aircraft dropped 2 bombs near Bn. Hd. Qr. Inter-company relief carried out.	
	17.		Hostile artillery very active throughout morning & afternoon. No casualties. 1 Platoon of Americans attached to each Company.	
	18.		Hostile artillery again very active. Working parties had to cease work at night. Retaliation asked for & obtained.	
	19		Quieter day. Enemy aircraft dropped 3 bombs in vicinity of Bn. Hd. Qr.	
	20		Fairly quiet day. Battalion relieved by 2/10th Londons moved into Bde. Support	
	21 22 23		Quiet days. Working parties under R.E.	
	24		Quiet day. Heavy gas shelling at 8.15pm & at 1.15am (25.4)	
	25		Anglo raid carried out by Bn. from sector on right. Barrage put down on Bn. front	
C.6.C.5.3.	26		Bn. relieved by 24th Londons & moved into LAVIEVILLE - BAIZIEUX Sector. 2 Coys in dundees, 2 in billets	
	27 28		Cleaning up & baths. Working parties under R.E.	
	29		2 Companies in LAVIEVILLE exchanged with 2 Companies in BAIZIEUX	
	30		Battalion relieved by 4th Bn. London Regt. in Support position & Left Sub-Sector.	
	31		Quiet day. Working parties under R.E. 1 O.R. wounded.	

R.H. Lindsay Major
Commdg. Queen Victoria's Rifles.

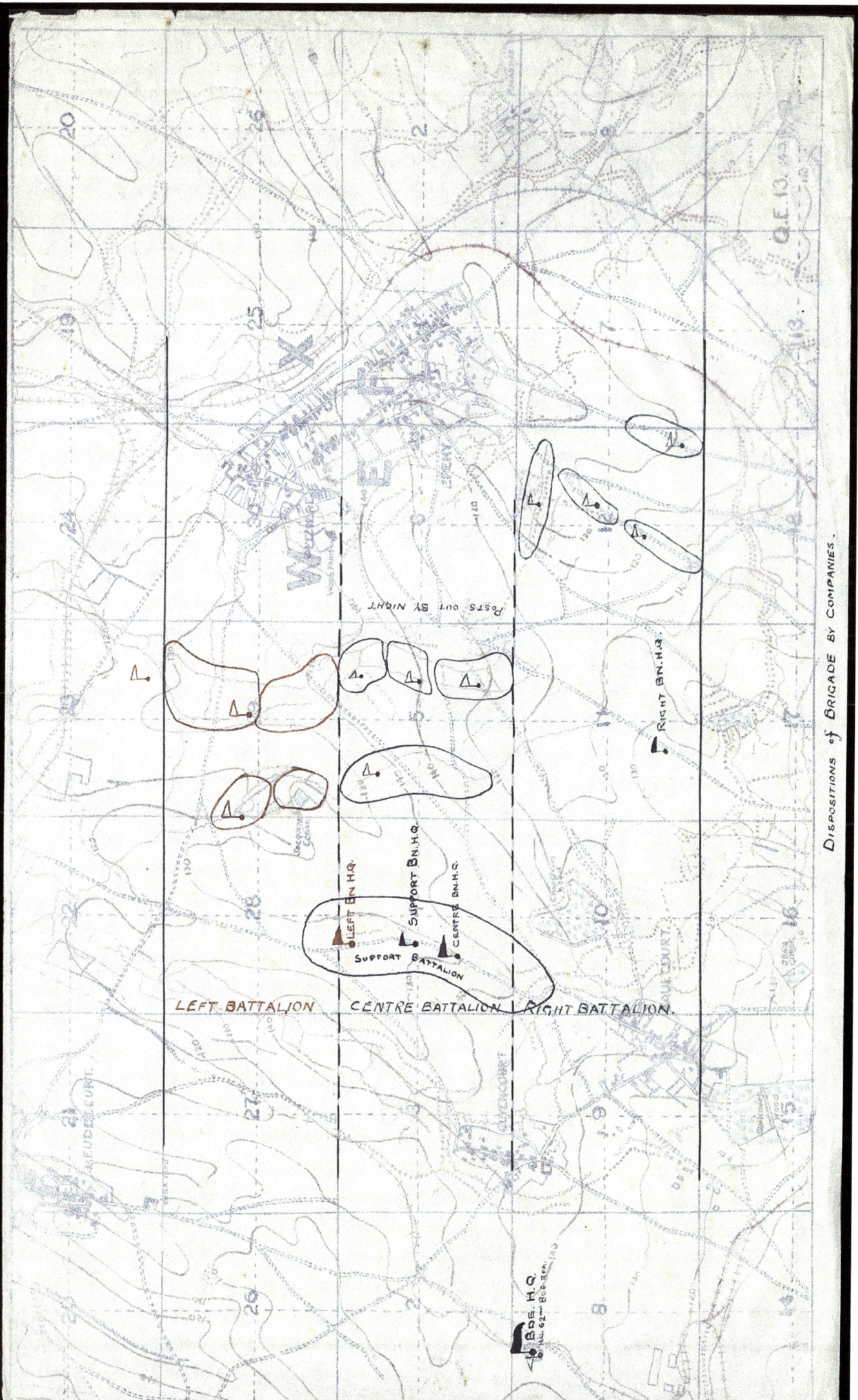

Марф "II"

175th Bde.

58th Div.

9th BATTALION

LONDON REGIMENT (QUEEN VICTORIA RIFLES)

AUGUST 1918

175/58

Vol 19

Confidential

War Diary
of
9th Battalion London Regiment
(Queen Victoria Rifles)

From 1st August 1918 to 31st August 1918

WAR DIARY or INTELLIGENCE SUMMARY

Army Form C. 2118.

9th London Regt. of Queen Victoria's Rifles

(Erase heading not required.)

Instructions regarding War Diaries and Intelligence Summaries are contained in F.S. Regs., Part II. and the Staff Manual respectively. Title pages will be prepared in manuscript.

Place	Date	Hour	Summary of Events and Information	Remarks and references to Appendices
DARWIN RESERVE TRENCH D14.23	Aug 1		Day quiet	62 D
	2		"	
	3		Battn relieved by 6th R.W. Kents (12th Divn) Bn marches to D13a5.4 on relief & embuses to VIGNACOURT.	57 E
VIGNACOURT	4		Battn arrives at 7 hrs. Day spent resting & cleaning up.	
"	5		B.G.C. inspects the Battn in the evening. Coy. Training	
"	6		Battn moves by bus to FRANVILLERS & then marches to BOIS ESCARDONNEUSE H.Q. at I5c70.15	62 D
BOIS ESCARDONNEUSE	7		Battn in Corps Reserve. C.O. + 2nd/Lt. with the B.G.C. reconnoitres roads to the front line. All fighting equipment made good in the Bn.	
	8		The offensive started. The Battn moves 2hq K + 175 B/T.M.B. ordered to move to occupy the BALLARAT - ROMA "LINE", arriving there at 15.30 hours & occupies trench from J15c 7.7 to J22 d 6.3 Battn H.Q. at J22 a 5.2 (in reserve at the disposal of 18th Divn.) At 17 hours ordered to move up to K31a in support to 173 Inf/Bde who were attacking at 19h. The attack owing to casualties failed. The C.O. appreciated the bad situation immediately moved B.C. + D. Coys forward to E end of MALLARD WOOD (K27.33) reinforcing the elements of 173rd, 174th Bdes + held that line. "B" left Coy "C" centre "D" right. "A" Coy in reserve line approx K26d 4.6 to K26d 6.2 (defensive flank) Battn H.Q. at K26 3.6.3 Patrols from K33 a 6.8 & K33d 5.6 (battery of half guns) K33 c 9.7. K33 3 4.5. K33 a 2.9. 1 officer 20 R.s were captured during this operation. We were under the command of B.G.C. 173rd Bde at the time.	

R.M. Lindsay Bn.Lr Mjr
(comdg) 9th Battn LONDON REGT
(QUEEN VICTORIA'S RIFLES)

Army Form C. 2118.

WAR DIARY
or
INTELLIGENCE SUMMARY

9th London Bat. Queen Victorian Rifles

(Erase heading not required.)

Place	Date	Hour	Summary of Events and Information	Remarks and references to Appendices
MALLARD WOOD	9th		Heavy shelling of the Battn area. At 15 hours orders arrived to withdraw to training K31F to be in reserve to an attack. Great 11/30 hours. Small posts had to be left to cover the retirement. At 17.2 hours the Battn had assembled at the place during the garrisons of these posts. The attack was successful but heavy casualties to the 12th Battn also old Americans on their right demanded reinforcements. The Battn immediately moved forward at 20 hrs. "C" Coy reinforced the Rangers on their objective K19 central to K11 2 3 0. "A" Coy formed defensive flank facing SE on line K17c 8 9 b. K17c 6 6. B & D Coys in support on line K16a 6 & K12d 9 1. Battn H.Q. at K21 E 6 5. The casualties sustained during that operation was slight. Capt. F.H. Rawles M.C. assumed command of the Battn. K9th Eqn POWERS to command 75th D. Bde.	62 D
BOIS DE TAILLES	10th		Report from Frank Battn Col R15 "C" Bat. Points that here in position at boundary at Bofat. AMIENS defence line at K5d R16 B-d + K24 b + was there necessary to occupy that line from (K12 b-d) from K6 c 5 2 to K12d 8 6. Patrols were sent forward. Receive "G" Coy was sent forward. Much opposition was encountered heavy artillery & MG fire. "B" Coy went south to reinforce "C" Company MG's. Bridge on left it was obvious that the left flank Battn. (12th Divn) were not in K5 also reported "A" Coy moved west to form defensive flank being NE diggings on line K11 a.n. to K.17 B 3 about to cover the advance of the C Coys. "A" Coy however received from K7 central to K11 a 30. At 16 30 hrs were on objective in touch with 13 2 WSh on right but not on left. Known nth 12th Divn found that opposition had been to strong that an attack was taking place on touch in K5a C+a at 18 hours information was immediately sent forward. The retreating enemy were many casualties inflicted. The Bn gained objectives K17 a top of 700 yard. We still retain their causalties. During the operation Germans resembled approx. 30 + 50 ORs. Battn H.Q. on K19 a 7 5. R.H. Rawles R.

WAR DIARY or INTELLIGENCE SUMMARY

Army Form C. 2118.

9th London Regt / Queen Victoria's Rifles

Place	Date	Hour	Summary of Events and Information	Remarks and references to Appendices
BOIS DE TAILLES	11th		2nd R.B. Div. on left occupied the gap between ourselves & the books on left. Very heavy Patrol quiet in the a.m. Shelling of Bois area. Also M.G. Sniper very active. Patrol by "B" Coy found the enemy's Sniper's Posts about 150 yds N of Triangle & returning N.15.c.4.7 a+b.	62 D
	12th		Day Quiet. 58th Div. relieved by 147 & London div. the 2/2nd replaced Q.V.Rs. Battn moved into reserve in area J.16.c.7.8. under bivouacs for the night	
BOIS ESCARDONNEUSE	13th		Battn moved to BOIS ESCARDONNEUSE T.31.a Battn H.Q. at T.31.a.6.7.	
	14th		Baths, cleaning up, bathing etc. Major R.M. Lindsey-Renton assumed Command of the Battn.	
	15th		Cleaning up. Coy training.	
	16th		Training	
	17th		Inspection by Field Marshal Sir Douglas Haig during training.	
	18th		Church parade + Training. B.G.C. Conference of all officers	
	19th		Training	
	20th		"	
	21st		" Btn under orders to move in 1 hour notice from 19 hours.	
	22nd		15th L/Cple left BOIS ESCARDONNEUSE at 14.45 hrs. marched via BONNAY MERICOURT + TREUX + occupied trenches in old front line Q.V.Rs. with 1 Coy R.F.a + Battn HQ at K.16.d.2.4. such orders to move at a moments notice. At 17 hrs message received saying Strong enemy Counter attack and 47 Div " And Bde to a.o Stand to. At 22 hrs orders to proceed at once + occupy the old AMIENS defence line from N.3d.6.6 to N.12.2.7. the 12th Battn. right 2/10 th in Reserve.	

R.M. Lindsey-Renton
Major
Comm'g 9th BATTN LONDON REGT
(QUEEN VICTORIA'S RIFLES.)

Army Form C. 2118.

WAR DIARY
9th London Regt Queen Victoria's Rifles
or
INTELLIGENCE SUMMARY.

(Erase heading not required.)

Place	Date	Hour	Summary of Events and Information	Remarks and references to Appendices
	23rd		At 2.30am this was completed. D Coy left forward company from K5a.6.8 – K6c.20.15. B Coy right forward coy from K6c.20.15. – K12b.2.7. A Coy in support K5b.0.1.5. – K11c.4.9. C Coy in reserve in old line east K11c.2.3. Battn. H.Q at K9b.2.8.	
		11.30am	B. & C. Coys beginning of the Os. unless by my attack resumed to capture GREEN LINE which was held the final objective of 47th Divn. on previous day. One officer per coy nominated went from present position to jumping off point, which was approx 300x W J ALBERT–BRAY RD J and F.3.4.0.9. E railway L2a.5.2 thence S.W. 15 yards L8a.1.9. thence K L8a.2.0. This line was being held by 47th Divn. Coy Commanders advance including an officer T.M's & M.G.C. one metal, and plans for the attack examined and front advanced line reviewed. All companies had left position & moved up to tanks jumping off line At midnight Battn. H.Q. Junior at CUPSE L14.3.3.	
		11.15pm	At 12.50am. all companies were in position. A Coy left & D Coy night assembling company B Coy in support. C Coy in reserve minus 2 platoons one with each assembling coy for purpose of MOPPING UP HAPPY VALLEY F26b & c27c. I sect M.B.'s also T.M's advanced with Reserve coys to be used when front objective was reached, to consolidate. Battn. Left Boundary F26.0.3.2, Right Boundary L2 central. 47 Divn on left. RANGERS on right. ZERO 1am.	
	24th		At 2.30am the C.O. went forward and found D Coy in line along FRICOURT–BRAY RD F27.6.5.4–F.27.6.6.6. in touch with RANGERS on right but not in touch on left. C Coy was digging in on line K27a.9.2. –K27a.2.8. B platoon of B. Coy on rifle pits from K27a.9.4 – K27a.7.9. & 2 platoon forming a defensive flank facing N.W. along 2nd Trench K27a.9.7. K.27a.6.5.	

R.M Lodge Ponton Major
Commdy 9th Battn. LONDON. REGT.
(QUEEN VICTORIA'S RIFLES)

Army Form C. 2118.

9th London Regt. Queen Victoria Rifles.

WAR DIARY
or
INTELLIGENCE SUMMARY.
(Erase heading not required.)

Place	Date	Hour	Summary of Events and Information	Remarks and references to Appendices
	24.		A Coy could not be found however, at about 4pm they reported to be in New Trench about K21c 6.3 - K21c 2.2. and in Trench with 47th Div. They subsequently moved down & joined up with D Coy. Batln H.Q. moved up to L2 A85.90. and halts 1E HAPPY VALLEY K27c 39. The enemy was very active during the day and M.Gs and snipers & also whirling in region of HAPPY VALLEY & railway running W in L2 causing many casualties. M.Gs also tried to work up between Battns. but this was effectively stopped by 2/10th Londons, who pushed forward companies to fill up gaps.	
		1.52pm	Orders were received for Brigade to attack at 4pm. This was inevitably postponed until 2.30pm following morning. CAPT. F.H. RALLS M.C. was killed during the 2/Lieuts Jenny and the fight with the C.O. Casualties up to 15th this front had been about 150 O.Rs & 6 Officers. C.O. held Coy Comdrs Conference at 9pm and issued instructions for the attack. B Coy left front bay. & B Coy right front bay. A Coy Supps. D reserve. The Battn. was relieved by 15th Ldns (47th Dn) at about midnight 24/25th and	
	25.		moved to assembly positions E of FRICOURT-BRAY RD. left flank resting on X rds K27d 5.5.45. right flank K27d 8.3. 15th LONDONS on left 2/10 LDNs on RIGHT. Barrage commenced at 2.30am and troops moved forward. Batln H.Q. moved to K27b 6.3 at 3am. As many slack ground must prevailed from the time message was received from Capt W.E. BOWLER (B Coy) reporting that he was consolidating along road running S.E. from BRONFAY FARM K27d. Am. was not in touch with people on right and only about 16 of the 15th LONDONS on the left. Realising his situation, his strength at 30 rifles. The C.O. immediately moved forward & formed D Coy plus M.G.s + a Coy of 2/2 Londons in line facing N.E. about K29c centre. At this time the west was	

Army Form C. 2118.

Instructions regarding War Diaries and Intelligence Summaries are contained in F. S. Regs., Part II. and the Staff Manual respectively. Title pages will be prepared in manuscript.

9th London Regt. WAR DIARY

Queen Victoria's Rifles

INTELLIGENCE SUMMARY.

(Erase heading not required.)

Place	Date	Hour	Summary of Events and Information	Remarks and references to Appendices
	Aug 25		Q.V.R's were disposed as follows: B Coy from K30a25g5 – K30a35b0. C Coy K30a35b0 – K30a45.20. A Coy K29b9u – 9.0. D Coy were being sent forward to reI Kanche N.W of BRONFAY FARM VK29d. 173 were pushed through in During the morning and 1/4 Bde South in the afternoon. Our casualties in this attack were about 3 Offrs 70 O.Rs. The Battn moved back to valley F28d into bivouac Bn HQ at F28a3.2.	
	26		Day spent resting.	
	27		Battn moved to junction of trenches in F28c in old trenches at 12 noon. Officers reconnoitred SHEFFIELD AV in A20a (b2c) 1st defence position.	
	28		Battn returned to 9th LDNS in newly captured position from A17d95 – SUPPORT COPSE A24a. B & D Coy in front lines to the centre A27a55 – A27a3500. Bn H.Q. at A23.5.36. A Coy during the night pushed forward on outpost line running A18a77 – A18d 4.0. From observation it was apparent that the BOSCHE had gone back, patrols could not locate him at all. At 4.20 p.m. orders were received to move at once to occupy Kanche running S.W from MAUREPAS, in B14d – 20 central. A B & D companies occupied this line with C Coy in support at from B14c54 – A14c 6.0.	
	Sept 30		Bn.H.Q. at A20a26g5. Move complete by 6.30pm. Orders received at 3am to hold ourselves in readiness to move forward as MAIN GUARD in an advance guard action. About noon Bn received orders to proceed forward. 1/2 Duke of Suffolks (right) 5/10 Londons (right) in front and. R.M. Linssen Capt. 2nd in Command 9th Battn. London Regt. QUEEN VICTORIA'S RIFLES. ROUEN	

D. D. & L., London, E.C.
(A.1060) Wt W5500/P713 750,000 2/15 Sch. 52 Forms/C2118/16

WAR DIARY
or
INTELLIGENCE SUMMARY

Army Form C. 2118.

9th London Regt
Queen Victoria's Rifles

Place	Date	Hour	Summary of Events and Information	Remarks and references to Appendices
	Aug 30		Q.V.Rs (less RANGERS(right) in rear. Movement was made in artillery formation. Our companies were distributed as follows:- A&D in front B&C in rear. The advance was due EAST. the objection of SUFFOLKS & 2/10th being the high ground running N & S. in B.18 - B.24 central. The 9th & 12th Battns moved thro' at some strength and MOPPED UP MARRIERES WOOD and established themselves on the high ground in C.13+06 & C.19pt. The Batt. advanced with very few casualties, the SUFFOLKS & 2/10th established themselves on their objective. M.G's from W.corner of MARRIERES WOOD made it impossible to advance over the ridge. careful reconnaissance was made & the enemy appeared to be holding the wood in some strength. T.M's were very active and the trench in the wood running N & S in C.19a appeared to be wired. This information was sent to Bde. - plans were made for an attack and a barrage of ½ hr duration.	
	31		At 1.30am orders were received which stated that the Q.V.R's would withdraw the reserve alphs along gun line dividing squares B17 & 18 & 23 & 24 and that 174 Bde would pass through 175 Bde and capture MARRIERES WOOD & high ground beyond. The withdrawal of Battn was completed and the old trenches & gunpits were reoccupied. Batt H.Q being at approx B24a 1.3. At 2 pm orders were received to be ready for an attack with 174 Bde when was cancelled at about 4 pm and at 7.20 pm orders were received to proceed to S.E. corner of MARICOURT where guides would conduct the Batt. into Bivouacs, leaving guides to bring in 7th Div. & men vacated dug outs. 11.30 pm move completed. Battn. being in valley A 29a central.	

R.A. Lawson, Major a/c? Com'd 9th BATTN. LONDON REGt.
(QUEEN VICTORIA'S RIFLES)

175/58

War Diary.
9th London Regt:
September 1918.

32ND DIVISION
Pioneers
M.G.C.

September 1918

Confidential

WAR DIARY
- of -
9th Battn. LONDON REGIMENT (QUEEN VICTORIA'S RIFLES)
from 1st September 1918 to 30th September 1918

(Volume 1)

9th Battn. London Regt. (Queen Victoria's Rifles)

WAR DIARY
INTELLIGENCE SUMMARY.

Army Form C. 2118.

Place	Date	Hour	Summary of Events and Information	Remarks and references to Appendices
FARNY	1/9/18		Battalion resting and making shelters	
	2			
	3		Training etc.	
	4			
	5		Lieut Col E.G.H. POWELL met with an accident - Major R H LINDSEY-RENTON assumed command of the Battalion	
	6		Battalion moved up by Bus to D 20.d 1.5. (@ 62 C.NE) 140th Brigade (47th Division) on the line. The Battalion relieved the 1/5th London pbrs. complete Company of the 2nd Londons.	
			A Coy. relieved A and B Coys of 15th Londons - D 18.b.3.4. - D 18.d.3.8	
			B " " C and D " " D 18.d.3.8 - D 18.d.1.1	
			C " " 21st Londons D 18.d.1.1 - D 24.b.0.55	
			D " recupied trench D 18.2.3.3.	
			Battn H.Q at D 17.d.0.1	
			2/10th Battn London Regt on left - 74th Division on right. Relief complete at 1 am.	
	7	8 am	Battalion advanced line during early morning to get into line with french Battn - 8 am. Battalion attached in conjunction with french Battalions to Bell up for move down on line E 14.b.5.5 - E 28.c.3.5 by all C. pre post SAUCOURT Wood E 15 central - Artillery derit not too and attack proved furious. Opposition offered the further the Battn advanced until line of railway on E 18.d. 2 and 6 was reached. Left flank could not push on first. BAPRON COPSE in E 17.b. 2.5 up the reserve Coy filled the gap between them and our left flank E 18.b.6.0. Battn. H.Q established at E 16.d.5.9. Battn pushed forward at dusk by a series of strong patrols, and aft	

WAR DIARY or INTELLIGENCE SUMMARY

Army Form C. 2118.

Page 2

Place	Date	Hour	Summary of Events and Information	Remarks and references to Appendices
	7		overcoming opposition occupied line of trench running S.E. from railway E.18.b.9.w. to road F.19.b.2.9. about the 2 Coy of 12th Battn. Bridor Regt in support occupied trench from CAPRON COPSE E.10 E.18.b.6.4. the 2/10th Battn. also pushed forward to trench running E.18.a and c and E.18.a. Total casualties for day 7+400 yards Casualties 3 Officers and 116 O.R.	
	8		The 74th Division extended their boundary N to E and W line through E.12.c.o.o. The 5/5 Division extended their to E and W line through Pt.24.2.00 (57 c.5.E). The 74th Division pushed through as ordered and the 74th Brigade took over the Duremont front. The Battn. moved back to area E.2.d. and took over trenches. H.Q at E.2.d.9.6.	
	9	10am	Battn. ordered to stand to. This order was cancelled at 11am. Day spent cleaning and resting.	
	10		The situation forward was obscure. Battn. formed its own protection during the night. 1 Coy. outpost Coy. All entrances to BUYENCOURT prepared, also valley in E.3.a. but situation remained quiet.	
	11		Battn. relieved 2 Coys. of the 12th Battn. in the line — B Coy. left forward Coy. E.5.b.6.9.— E.5.b.7.5.4.5. D " centre " E.5.b.7.5.4.5. — E.5.d.6.7 C " right " E.5.d.6.7. — E.5.d.9.0 A " support Coy. Trench E.5.a.v.c. Battn. H.Q in E.r.c.5.5	
			2/10th Battn. on right. 12th Battn on left. 2/2nd Battn. in reserve.	
	12		Heavy hostile artillery fire on Brigade front from 9.30 to 10.30 am. Left of Battalion's front not reached by the enemy, and garrisons occupied. W. Coy O. Burnen Capt + adj	

8TH. BATTN. LONDON REGT.
(QUEEN VICTORIA'S RIFLES.)

Army Form C. 2118.

Page 3

WAR DIARY
or
INTELLIGENCE SUMMARY.

(Erase heading not required.)

Instructions regarding War Diaries and Intelligence Summaries are contained in F. S. Regs., Part II. and the Staff Manual respectively. Title pages will be prepared in manuscript.

Place	Date	Hour	Summary of Events and Information	Remarks and references to Appendices
	12		and surface-culture. Casualties 1 Officer and 5 O.R.	
	13		Day quiet. Hostile artillery active during the evening round SUPPORT TRENCH area. Identifications of each Coy relieved by one platoon of A Coy 2/24 London, who came into the line for instructions. The relieved platoons came back today. E.4, 6, 7, Y and formed one Coy under O.C. 2/24. Our artillery (all calibres). T.Ms, M.Gs, and gas C.E R.E bombarded EPEHY during the night. No retaliation.	
	14		Day quiet. The 4 platoons of this Battalion under the 2/24 Battalion proceeded to join their Coys, and the Coy of the 2/24 returned to their unit. The 12th Battalion on the left were relieved by the 1/4 Suffolks and moved into reserve relieving the 2/24 Battn, who returned to the 173rd Brigade.	
	15		The 174th Brigade relieved the 175th Brigade in the line. the Post Office Rifles relieved this Battn. A Coy relieved A.C.9. B Coy relieved B.Coy 70. Our guides met incoming Battn at 8.30 pm. at E.10 a 3.5. Relief complete at 10.45 pm. Our relief Battn moved to Camp at D 8 d. "All Corps no by 3 am. Battn H.Q at D 14 E. Y 9.	
	16			
	17		Battn cleaning up.	
	18	7 am	The 175th Brigade moved into Corps reserve no given E.2.b & 9. Battn being	
	19		billeted in area E.2 b and d. Battn H.Q at E.9.C 3.Y	

8TH. BATTN. LONDON REGT.
(QUEEN VICTORIA'S RIFLES.)

WAR DIARY or INTELLIGENCE SUMMARY

Army Form C. 2118.

Page 4

Place	Date	Hour	Summary of Events and Information	Remarks and references to Appendices
	20		The 175th Brigade relieved the 173rd Brigade on the line. 4/24th Battn relieving the 1/24th Battn. H.Q. at X.25.a.25.30 (57c). Companies disposed as follows:- Left front Coy. A at X.26.a.9.9 - X.26.b.25.25 Right " B " X.26.b.25.25 - X.26.c.9.8 Left support D " X.26.a.05.95 - X.25.b.9.8 Right " C " X.25.b.9.8 - X.25.b.5.8	
	21		The 2/10th Battn and 12th Battn passed through this Battn to obtain - owing to heavy casualties and opposition they were forced back almost to our line.	
	22		Battn attacked at 9.30 pm on a front of 700 yards and carried the enemy defences to a depth of 1500 yards in heavy rain, reaching final objective. KILDARE LANE - HOLTS TRENCH - KILDARE POST and DADOS LANE as far as X.22.d.3.4. 4 M.Gs were captured. Enemy commenced bombing along DADOS LANE about 11 am. After a short bombing fight he was ejected, leaving 2 killed and 2 wounded prisoners in our hands.	
	23		Battn was relieved by 9th Royal Fusiliers (Junior Division belonged to 2nd Anzac Division) (12th Division) and marched to VILLERS FAUCON	
	24		Battn entrained at VILLERS FAUCON at 6 am for TRONES WOOD area, arriving at	

9th BATTN. LONDON REGT.
(QUEEN VICTORIA'S RIFLES.)

WAR DIARY
or
INTELLIGENCE SUMMARY.

(Erase heading not required.)

Army Form C. 2118.

Page 5

Place	Date	Hour	Summary of Events and Information	Remarks and references to Appendices
	24	8.30 am	Day spent in resting	
	25		Day spent in cleaning up	
	26		Division being transferred to VIII Corps. Battn marched to DERNANCOURT and entrained for AUBIGNY (NW of ARRAS)	
	27		Battn detrained at AUBIGNY and marched to CAMBLAIN L'ABBÉ, being billeted at Hyder Camp.	
	28		Day spent in cleaning up and baths. C.O. and Coy Commanders reconnoitred line W. of LENS.	
	29		Church Parade and rest.	
	30		Battn entrained for line at 3 pm. Battn relieving 9th Royal Sussex 12 m (174th Division) Battn HQ at M.17.c.75.50. Coys as follows:-	
			Left front Coy A	
			Right do B	
			Left support Coy C	
			Right support Coy D	

(Received from Mrs Yarsey and put with Diary 7th July 1937. S.W.)

Q.V.R. (9/London Regt).

Copy of personal notes on operations from

August 12th. 1918.

to

September 26th. 1918.

From Major W.H.Lindsay-Renton,DSO.,TD.,

-o-o-o-o-o-o-o-o-o-o-o-o-o-o-o-o-

Reference 1. Notes on operations etc of Q.V.R. between August 12th
France.
62nd N.E.   and September. 26th.
1/20000.

After the action in Malard Wood and Tailes Wood the battalion
withdrew for a night to the neighbourhood of Square J.18 and from
there back on the following day to the Bois Escardonneuse on
August 13th. to tents and bivouacs, while in the area training
was carried out, the men washed, clothing and equipment were
cleaned up

N.B.
Captain Rolls M.C., who had been in command for most of these operations
was awarded the bar to the M.C.
Lieut.-Colonel Powell went on leave on August 11th.

On August 17th the Commander-in-Chief visited the 175th
Bde. and saw the Bn. carry out a practice counter-attack. In
the course of a conversation he laid very great stress on the
following principle:- Always throw in reinforcements and reserves
into places where progress is being made and not into places
where you are held up. The further you progress where you are
successful the more difficult it will be for the enemy to hold
out in the other places

During this period 2/Lt.Powell and a platoon from D.Coy.
gave a musketry demonstration to the brigade with tracer bullets
with special to the fire power of a platoon where fire control
and fire discipline is good. This demonstration went off very
well and was very interesting.

While the battalion had been resting the division (58th)
had carried out an attack on the Happy Valley which was successful at first but a counter attack drove the assaulting troops
back to a line W of the Leaulte-Bray road through F.19, 25 & 26 &
L.2.

In view probably of the possibility of the enemy making a
further counter-attack the 175th Bde. was ordered up to the
Amiens defence line (E of Tailes Wood). The Battalion went on
the left of the line with its left flank on the railway at
K 5 d 6.8 and its right flank on the track at K 12 b 2.7.

The Rangers (12th London) were on the right with the 10th
London in reserve. Troops of the 47th Division were in front
where the line had ended after the attack on Happy Valley, and
also on the left.

D Coy (left) and B Coy (right) were in front in the Amiens
defence system. A Coy in close support from K 5 d 1.5 to
K 11 b 4.9 and C Coy in reserve in K 11 b & d. Battn.H.Q. in
some old dug outs at K 17 b 2.8. At this time Captain Mayer
commanded A Coy, Captain Bowler B, Lieut.Hodgson C and Lieut.
McAdam D.

It is interesting to note that at this period the three
battalions in the 175th Bde. were all commanded by officers of
the Q.V.R. the 10th being under Major J.Nichols M.C. in the
absence of Lt.-Col. Cawston, and the 12th under Major S.Sampson,
M.C. in the absence of Lieut.Colonel C.Lait.

On August 23rd orders were received that the 175th Bde.
+ see map   would attack the light ground + E of Happy Valley. The attack
for object- was to be carried out by the Q.V.R. on the left, Rangers (12th)
ives etc.   on the right and 10th in reserve. Troops of the 47th Division
were attacking on the left and the attack would bring the line
up to that held by the Australians whose left flank was in the
neighbourhood of the Chalk Quarry in L 3 d.

The main difficulty of the attack was Happy Valley a deep valley about 100 yards to 300 yards wide with steep high banks on the W and E sides. This valley was known to be full of dug outs where the enemy could take refuge from our barrage. The success of the enemy's counter-attack at the previous attempt was reported to be due to a number of the enemy emerging from these dug outs and so getting the attacking troops from behind.

To deal with this one company of the 10th were attached to each of the assaulting battalions for "Mopping Up". In addition the Civil Service Rifles (15th) London of the 47th Division were detailed to follow in rear of the Bde. to mop up the valley from + N to S.

+ whether N to S or S to N?

During the afternoon of the 23rd officers went up and reconnoitred the area for assembly which was to be just behind the front line as then held. This was reported to be as shewn by the dotted line on map. The reconnaissance however showed that the line was a hundred or two yds. further west.

About 11.30 p.m. the battalion moved up to the assembly area and battalion HQ. was established at L 1 b 2.2 where also were the HQ of the 10th and 12th.

Owing to the brightness of the moon I feared that the enemy would see the troops assembling for the attack and cause considerable trouble and many casualties. In fact the enemy's machine guns were very active especially on the left in front of A Coy. who had some difficulty in getting into position and it is probable that he did see movement even if he did not put it down to an impending attack.

At 1 a.m. on the 24th the barrage came down and the attack started.

The battalion attacked in the following formation:-

A Coy (left) and D Coy. (right) in the first wave to take the actual objective laid down for the battalion, B Coy. (left) and C Coy. (right) in the second wave having as their task the digging of a support line on the reverse side of the high ground running through F 27 central. One platoon from each of these coys was attached to the leading wave to deal with any immediate mopping-up required until the arrival of the Coys. from the 10th, when they were to rejoin their Coys. The Coys. of the 10th attached to the battalion followed in rear of the 2nd wave.

Considerable opposition was met with in the Happy Valley and some stiff fighting took place. A Coy, in trying apparently, to keep touch with the 47th Div, who had edged off to the left a considerable distance, left a gap between their right and the left of D Coy. and when B Coy. came up in the second wave several machine guns were causing trouble. These were rushed and their crews killed. Captain Bowler did considerable execution in the fighting also Sergts. Ridgeley, Keats and Dunn. On the right D Coy. had a similar experience and 2/Lt. Powell caused the enemy many casualties.

After the valley had been captured the mopping-up was carried on with under difficulties owing to the night being much darker and the dugouts difficult to find (I did hear later that 100 prisoners were captured here more than 24 hours afterwards though there were a large number of troops in and moving through the valley) throughout the 24th.

The situation when the battalion started consolidating was as follows:-

A Coy. as mentioned above had gone off to the left. B Coy. being unable to find either A Coy. or the 47th Division, who were still some distance to the left of A Coy, had two platoons in an old trench which ran through F 27 a & b forming a defensive flank facing N. The + remainder of this Coy. dug in in F 27 a in touch with C Coy. on their right, a large gap existed between C and the 12th. D Coy. had reached the road running N & S through F 27 b & d and were not in touch on either flank. The enemy still had some men in the trench and 2/Lt. Powell captured a machine gun and crew of six in the trench.

+whether mopping up platoon still with A Coy?

At dawn Bn.HQ. (as well as those of the 10th and 12th) moved forward to the Forked Tree L 2 b 05.95 in accordance with Bn. orders. In the early hours of the morning difficulty was experienced in organizing the position satisfactorily as on both flanks troops finding themselves isolated and close to enemy machine guns and snipers - who were very active throughout the day and owing to the open nature of the country and the close range made all movement dangerous and caused some casualties - began to move back. This movement was stopped and later in the morning the situation became as follows:-

The Battalion of the 47th Division on the left in response to Captain Mayers request moved down to the right. A Coy. was thus enabled to move to the right also though it was still mostly in the 47th Division area. Posts were pushed out between A & B Coys. to connect up. One company from the 10th came forward to the road and filled up the gap between D Coy - who were rather in the position where A should have been - and the 12th.

This line was held for the rest of the 24th but would - but for subsequent events - have been adjusted in accordance with original plan under cover of darkness.

During the early hours of the morning Bn.HQ. was subjected to a heavy and sustained fire from 5.9 & 8" hows. The position being near the junction of the sunken roads and a railway was an obvious mark and was in addition under observation, from high ground from the direction of Trigger Wood and Ceylon Wood to the E. It would have been impossible, there being little or no cover, to remain there without incurring heavy casualties and Bn. HQ. was therefore (as were those of the 10th and 12th) moved to the east bank of Happy Valley. This place was also kept under continual shell fire throughout the day but some protection was afforded by the bank.

At about 1.40 p.m. on the 24th orders were received that the attack would be resumed at 4 p.m. the same day. These orders had been considerably delayed in reaching Bn.HQ. A conference was held with company commanders at B.Coy. HQ. and orders hurriedly issued. In view of the fact that the assembly had to take place in the open and under continual sniping and M.G. fire it was impossible to form up in a really suitable formation. Great difficulty was in fact experienced in assembling.

As no barrage came down at 4 p.m. as arranged, I enquired of Major Sampson commanding the 12th whether he knew what was the matter and was informed that the attack was postponed. The official orders as to the postponement only reached Bn. HQ. at 5.15 p.m.

Had the attack not been postponed it was, I think, in great danger of being a failure. The short time available, the necessity for assembling in the open by daylight with the enemy close at hand and the fact that the Bn. was not properly reorganized and could not be same under cover of darkness all militated against the success of the operation.

During the afternoon the Battalion suffered a great loss in the death of Captain Ralls who was hit by a sniper when accompanying me to the conference in connection with the attack.

The postponed attack was ordered for 2.30 a.m. on the morning of the 25th. The objective of the attack was to pass over the Gully E of Happy Valley and capture Bronfay Farm and the trenches E of it. The attack was carried out by all three battalions of the Brigade, Q.V.R. on the left, 10th in the centre, and Rangers on the right. The Civil Service Rifles (15th London) of the 47th Division were attacking on the left and the Australians on the right.

The objective given to the Battalion was the line between Billon Copse and Bronfay Wood.

The battalion assembled for the attack on both sides of the road running N & S through F 27 b & d. The assembly was carried out undisturbed and at 2.30 a.m. the barrage came down and the attack commenced. The battalion attacked in the following formation B (left) C (right) in the front line to capture the actual objective D Coy. and A Coy (the latter under 2/Lt.Powell in the absence of Captain Mayer who was wounded on the morning of the 24th) in support to make a support line in a suitable position in the neighbourhood of Bronfay Farm.

Very little opposition was met with from the enemy but some difficulty was encountered at first in getting to the objective owing, at first, to the fact that the gully E of Happy Valley was difficult to cross having high and very steep banks also the gully having several turns in it tended to throw the troops off their direction, and then, and mainly, owing to the fact that a thick mist came down making it impossible to see more than a few yards. At first units got mixed up and were ignorant as to where they were and as to the position of troops on their flank. In a short time however they were organized and pushed forward to the objective which was occupied along the whole Brigade front. The battalion was distributed as follows:-
B & C Coys. in the old trenches between Billon Copse and Bronfay Wood; A Coy. just in rear in the trenches immediately S.E. of Bronfay Farm & D Coy. who had started consolidating some distance back were brought up to the trenches immediately N.W. of Bronfay Farm.

Early on the morning of the 25th units of the 173rd Bde. which had been closely following up the attack and sending out patrols, went through the 175th Bde. and carried on with the attack. Considerable opposition was met with from Billon Wood.

Bronfay Farm and its neighbourhood were subjected to heavy shell fire throughout the day including gas shells but despite the bad condition of the trenches mostly shallow and wide the casualties were not many.

In the afternoon orders were received that the battalion would be relieved that night by the Post Office Rifles (8th London) of the 174th Brigade and on relief would occupy Bivouacs and huts in the gully in L 28 c & d. The night was extremely dark and rain fell heavily throughout the night so that the battalion did not get back until well into the early hours of the 26th.

The battalion had then in two night attacks advanced the line to a distance of nearly 4500 under the difficulties which arose from darkness and the nature of the ground. These were overcome by careful use of the compass and excellent work by Company Officers and N.C.O's. In the attack on the evening of 23/24th the battalion met with considerable opposition and took many prisoners and killed a number of the enemy. In the attack on the morning of the 25th the battalion attacked after a very trying 24 hours conditions which made their success creditable if only for the difficulty in keeping direction and finding their objective.

The battalion stayed in the gully resting until the afternoon of the 27th when orders were received to go forward and occupy the trenches between Billon Farm and Contour Wood where they remained until the following evening. This period was without any occurrence of interest.

Ref:-
France
sheet
62 c N,W.
1/20000.

On the morning of the 28th verbal orders were received that the 175th Bde. with the 1/4th Suffolks (Pioneers) attached would relieve the 173rd and 174th Bdes. that evening in the trenches E of Maricourt which had been the German front line system in 1916 before the opening of the Battle of the Somme. The Suffolks were to be on the left holding the Bois d'En Haut (A 18), Q.V.R. from their right to Support Copse with a laison post there with the 12th the next battalion, with the 10th on the extreme right.

On receipt of the above orders I proceeded with Captain Duncan (the Adjt) and reconnoitred the line. We found that the Brigades in the line had just carried out an attack and the situation was far from clear and it was exceedingly difficult to find how to take over the line.

It took a considerable time to find any Bn.H.Q., and to select the battalion which appeared to be holding the sector to be taken over.

Eventually I decided to relieve the 3rd London (173rd Bde) who appeared to be according to account to be the only battalion in the sector. Their most forward company was in the trench running N & S through A 17 d 85.00 to A 17 d 85.60.

Arrangements were made for the relief and on my return to Bn.HQ. a proportion of officers and N.C.O's were sent up to get to their trenches by daylight in order to get a good idea as to their trenches before dusk.

During the afternoon written orders for the relief were received and those showed the front line as being a good thousand yards ahead of where it had been pointed out to me. I explained this at a conference at Bde. HQ. that evening and received instructions that if the line was not held by the other Bde., I was to push forward a company before dawn and establish an outpost line there overlooking the valley running though Jigsaw Copse (B.13.d) and Battery Copse (B.20 a & c).

Just before the Bn. marched off a wire was received that the Bdes. in the line had orders from the Div. to push forward to the outpost line before relief. This had not been done when the Bn. took over.

While the relief was in progress and officer from the 2nd. London turned up and stated that a company of that battalion was in front of the 3rd London in the trench running N.W from Support Copse through A 24 a & A 18 c. Arrangements were made to alter the relief and to relieve the company. As soon as the relief was completed A Company under 2/Lt.P$_o$well was ordered to push forward and establish an outpost line in accordance with instructions received from Bde. This was done and at dawn A Coy. was dug in along the high ground in A 18 d and A 24 b. in touch with the Suffolks in Bois d'En Haut. Touch with the 12th was not got until daylight. This was a very satisfactory piece of work on the part of A Coy. in view of the difficulties which naturally arise in pushing forward nearly 1000 yards immediately after relief with no idea as to the enemy's position and in view of the short time available for the men to get out and dig themselves in by dawn.

The rest of the battalion was distributed as follows D on the left B on the right with 3 platoons each in the trench running N.W from Support Copse with a platoon each in Support in the trench running N & W through A 17 d 85.00 to A 17 d 85.60.

Later in the morning I received orders to attend a conference at B.H.Q. at 2 p.m. where I was informed that permission had been obtained to carry out the attack in the night.

The general plan was as follows :- The Div. - (?which) on the left were making an attack on Limerick Post with one company attacking from the W and one Coy. from the N from the direction of Meath Post (X 21 b) which was in our hands; at the same time the Q.V.R. were to attack Kildare Post from the W while a company of the 1/4th Suffolks (Pioneers) who were to be attached to the battalion would assemble in the neighbourhood of Catelet Copse (X 28 d) which was in British hands and attack from the S. A standing barrage of about 20 minutes to half an hour was arranged to be put on Kildare Lane & Kildare Post to lift off the N position - that portion in X 22 c - 12 minutes before it lifted off the remaining portion which was further E.

The assembly area was a N & S line through the junction of Kildare Avenue and the sunken road at X 27 a 3.9. the coy. of the division on the left assembling N of the junction the Q.V.R. S of the junction.

In view of the above orders another conference of company commanders had to be held and orders issued for the attack.

During the afternoon information was received that a company of the division on the left had attempted to take Limerick Post and had been driven back, later news was received that the head of the battalion in Kildare Avenue had withdrawn some distance down the trench in a westerly direction. This vitally affected the position of the Q.V.R. as if the enemy got into this trench he could bring an enfilade fire to bear upon the battalion as it attacked towards Kildare Post. Arrangements were therefore made for the troops in Kildare Avenue to push forward again.

Information was received in the evening from Lt.Crosbie commanding A Coy. that the Coy. who had failed to take Limerick Post reported the presence of German M.G. in front of the post and that in his opinion there were also M.G's firing from in front of Kildare Post.

Arrangements were hurriedly made with the Bde. to alter the barrage to deal with these guns. The barrage was accordingly arranged to come down 300 yds. W of the line of Trenches and then to creep back at the rate of 100 yds. in 4 minutes until it reached the trench line and then carry on as before.

Late in the afternoon the Coy. of Suffolks moved off to take up its assembly position and after dark the battalion took up its assembly position. At 9.30 p.m. the barrage came down and the attack started.

The battalion attacked as follows:- B Coy. on the left under Lt.Hodgson to capture Kildare Lane from the sunken road at X 22.c 3.1 to trench junction in X 28 a 70.95 then to work up Dados Lane and Dados Loop as far as its junction with Sprint Trench at X 22 d 45.00. On capturing this a block was to be established in Stone Trench; A Coy. on the right under Lt.Crosbie to capture remainder of Kildare Lane also Kildare Post and then work up Holts Trench and Sprint Trench and join up with B Coy, on completion of this to establish a block in Catelet Trench.

In support D Coy. on the left under Lt.McAdam to take over and mop up the portion of Kildare Lane captured by B Coy. and to hold this and a portion of Dados Lane, on the right C Coy. to act similarly with the remainder of Kildare Lane and Kildare Post and take over the portion of Holts Trench. The Coy. of Suffolks after assisting in the capture of Kildare Post were to hold the line of the sunken road running from X 28 central to Kildare Post.

The 175th Bde. were in Corps reserve round Guyencourt to which place the battalion moved at about 9 a.m. on the 18th. The disposition of the battalion was as follows:- B Coy. in the Sunken road running N.W. from Guyencourt through E 3 c & E 2 d, C Coy. in the trench N of this road in E 3 c, and D Coy. in the trench S of this road in E 9 a, and A Coy. in the Sunken road in E 2 c & E 8 a.

During the day orders were received that the battalion would remain in the area for the night but that the men could be put into huts etc. B & C Coys. accordingly were distributed in huts in Guyencourt A & D Coys. remaining in their previous positions.

The battalion stayed here for the 19th and on Sept. 20th received orders to take over the front line where the situation was that the 173rd Bde had taken Poplar Trench but the division on the flank had not gone sufficiently far forward to squeeze them out.

The battalion took over the sector as follows:-
A (left) B (right) in Poplar Trench and Fir Support, East of the Sunken road in X 26 a, C (under 2/Lt.Lavington, Captain Samuelson being on leave) and D (under Lt.McAdam) in support in Fir Support, W of the sunken road in X 26 a, and Beech Avenue. Bn. HQ. was established in the railway cutting about X 25 a /.2.

On the same night orders were issued that the 10th and 12th battns. were to attack Kildare Post X 28 b and the trenches in X 28 b & X 22 d. The plan was roughly that the 10th Battn. were to attack Kildare Post and the trenches around it whilst the 12th attacking in rear were to form a defensive flank along Kildare Avenue. The Q.V.R. received orders to put Bridges over Poplar Trench to enable the 12th, who were assembling in rear of the trench, to pass over. This was done by raising duck boards from the floor of the trench, which had been the English Front Line at some time before the German offensive, and laying them across the trench.

The attack started at 5 a.m. on the 21st under an artillery barrage but was unable to achieve its object. The two battalions came under heavy M.G. fire from both Kildare Post and also Limerick Post to the N. The survivors of the 10th with the 12th ended up in Kildare Avenue.

The battalion stayed in Poplar Trench during the 21st and in the evening D Coy went forward and dug posts in the bank of the Sunken road in X 27 a. They were exposed to a great deal of shelling and M.G. fire and suffered some casualties.

At about 7 a.m. on the morning of the 22nd orders were received that the battalion must be prepared to carry out the same attack on receipt of orders to move. A conference with Company Commanders was held at B Coy's H.Q., and orders issued.

Later in the morning the B.G.C. 175th Bde. came up to Bn. HQ. and said that the division wanted the attack to be carried out that day as soon as an attack which was taking place on Limerick Post had succeeded. (In view of the fact that it would be necessary to move the battalion forward in small parties in order to get to a jumping off place I asked for and was granted 3 hours notice before attacking). Should the attack on Limerick Post not come off that day the battalion would have to attack at night. I pointed out that it was known that there were machine guns in Kildare Post and that the enemy were still in possession of the high ground to the N and that an attack by daylight would be in grave danger of failing and asked that it might be carried out by night. The General agreed but said that orders from higher authority were urgent. I pressed him to ask again that it should be done at night.

In view of this conversation another conference of company commanders was held and orders issued for a night attack should that be decided on.

Late in the afternoon orders were received from the Bde. that the Battalion would withdraw at dusk. The battalion accordingly withdrew to trenches and huts on the W outskirts of Guyencourt.

On the evening of Sept. 10th while resting at Guyencourt information was received from the Bde. that the situation on the Divisional front was obscure and that the battalion must take steps for its own protection. A Coy. was therefore detailed to provide outposts round the village of Guyencourt. These outposts were withdrawn at 6 a.m.

On Sept. 11th the 175th Bde., with the 2/24th London Regt., who had recently arrived from Palestine and who had been put into the 173rd Bde, attached, received orders to take over the divisional front. The 12th London, who had been lent to the 173rd Bde. on the previous night and had been holding the trench system in W 29 & E 5 from the E & W grid line between squares W Z 3 & W 29 to the east and west grid between squares E 5 & E 11, side stepped to the left and occupied the trenches in W 29 only with a Coy. in Tottenham Post (W 30 c) the Q.V.R. took over the trenches evacuated by the 12th in E 5 and the 10th the trenches in E 12 a & b. The 2/24th were in reserve along the Sunken road in E 4 a & c.

The battalion took over the sector as follows:-
B (left) D (Centre) C (right) in the trenches in E 5 b & d with 3 platoons each in the front trench and one platoon in the support trench. A Coy. in reserve in the trench in E 5 a & c. Battn. HQ. was established in the Sunken road in E 4 c.

The tour of duty in this sector was fairly quiet on the battalion front and was quite a rest for the men after the frequent fighting and advancing.

On the morning of Sept. 12th the enemy put down a heavy barrage on the Bde. front which was intense on the front of the 12th, and shortly afterwards raided Tottenham Post and killed or captures most of the garrison. Shortly afterwards about 50 of the enemy were seen in Wood Farm just south of Tottenham Post and the artillery was put on to them. 100 rounds rapid fire from a battery was put on to this place and the enemy were not seen any more. (During this tour in the trenches 2/Lt. Adamson was killed by a shell).

Towards the end of the tour 4 platoons of the 2/24th and 4 of the Q.V.R. changed places to allow the Q.V.R. a rest and at the same time give the 2/24th an insight into warfare on the western front. This would have continued but the 2/24th were withdrawn from the Bde.

On Sept. 15th the battalion was relieved by the Post Office Rifles (8th London) of the 174th Bde., and moved back to bivouacs and tents in Ville Wood just W of the Nurlu Peronne road.

Nothing of interest occurred whilst the battalion was resting in the wood except that one night there was a gale and rainstorm of exceptional violence lasting over two hours. Numbers of tents were blown over and practically everything was soaked. It was the worse storm I have experienced for its intensity.

On Sept. 17th orders were received that an attack was to be made on Sept. 18th on Epéhy and Peziéres by the (?20th) Div. on the left the 58th Div. in the centre and the 12th Div. on the right. The general scheme was roughly that the 58th Div. were to pass forward through Peziéres and take Poplar Trench (x 26). The div. on the left and the 12th on the right were to attack at the same time and after the 58th had taken Poplar Trench the other divisions would push forward and the 12th would take over the front of the 58th which would be squeezed out. This attack met with considerable opposition both in Peziéres and Epéhy where a lot of hand to hand fighting took place but both these places were eventually carried by storm.

C Coy. in reserve in the old German front line in the vicinity of Battn.HQ. which were at A A 23 b 1.5 (approx).

No sign of the enemy could be seen at daybreak and it was believed that the enemy had withdrawn. Messages were also received that the Australians had entered Hindleg Wood (B 26 c & d) and that the division on the left was also pushing forward. The battalion received orders not to push forward until receipt of orders to do so.

Meanwhile Cavalry patrols were seen entering Maurepas from the S.E. (B 14 b). Followed shortly afterwards by Field Artillery and later heavy artillery towed by lorries.

+ 1 or 2?

In the late morning or early afternoon the Suffolks sent forward * 2 Coys. to occupy the trench running S.W. from Maupepas, and later the battalion received orders that the Suffolks were pushing forward to the trench running S.E. from Maurepas and that as soon as news was received that they had moved the rest of the Bde. would push forward. The 10th (12th?), (I am uncertain whether the 10th or 12th were on the right of the Q.V.R, but believe 12th with 10th in front) in the same trench as the Suffolks and on the right, the Q.V.R. and 12th (10th?) in the trench running S.W. from Maurepas with the Q.V.R. on the left with the brigade (and also divisional) boundaries as follows:- Northern boundary E & W line through B 14 b 0.0., sotuhern boundary E & W line through B 26 b 0.0.

News was shortly afterwards received from the Bde that the Suffolks had started moving and the battalion moved off. On arrival at the trench allotted to the battalion it was found that the Suffolks had not all gone forward and that some had not reached the trench yet. When all the Suffolks had advanced the battalion was distributed as follows A (left) D (centre) B (right) with 3 platoons each in the trench in question and one platoon each in support. C Coy. in reserve in shell holes and gun pits between the trench and the road running from S end of Maurepas through B 14 b & c and B 20 a.a.

The Battaltoñ stayed in the situation for the night of the 29th, and in the early morning about 3 a.m. orders were received that the advance would be resumed on the 30th and that the 175th Bde. with Cavalry, artillery and R.E. attached would form the advanced guard but that the main guard would not move forward until the van guard (cavalry) had reported on the situation. [As Lieut.-Colonel Powell arrived early that morning I received orders to go back to the Transport lines near Maricourt as battle surplus and therefore I know nothing more at the period than the fact that the Bde. moved forward in the direction of Marrieres Wood and that orders were received by the battalion to carry out an attack which eventually did not come off.]

On the 31st the division was relieved by the 74th Division and on the same day the battalion came back to rest in bivouacs and shelters in Fargny Wood (A 28 b A 29 a). While in this locality training was carried out and the men bathed etc.

During the period of rest Lt.General Godley then commanding the 3rd Corps paid a visit to the Headquarters of the 175th Bde. and congratulated battalion commanders on the splendid work done by their battalions.

On Sept. 5th Lt.-Colonel Powell had an accident, owing to a bridge over a branch of the Somme giving way under his horse, and had to go to hospital.

Ref:-
Map A.

On Sept. 6th the Bde. received orders to take over the line from the 47th Division. Officers were sent up to reconnoitre and at about 5 p.m. the battalion embussed and proceeding via Bouchavesnes (c 14) and Moislains (C 18) to the Nurlu-Peronne road.

This was unusually far forward for busses as the battalion HQ. of the battalion in the line was on this raod and the front line was only just east of Aizecourt-Le-Bas.

On arrival at the debussing point I proceeded to Bde. HQ. and learnt that the Brigade was to carry out an attack on the following morning. The attack was to be carried out by the 10th on the left, Q.V.R. on the right, and 12th in support. The objective for the battalion was the high ground just east of St. Emilie (F 13 c F 19 a) the 10th to continue the line to the N with the 12th Division on their left, and the 74th division were also attacking on the right. The advance to be made was over 7000 yds.

The line taken over by the Battalion on the night of the 6th was on Hill 145 (D 18 & 24) E of Aizecourt-Le-Bas, where battn. HQ. spent the night in a Nissen Hut, and was about 1000 yds. in rear of the line on both flanks. The battalion was therefore ordered to advance level to the general line before the attack started.

A section of 18 pounders, a machine gun section, and 2 Stokes Trench mortars were attached to the battalion.

The attack which was carried out without an artillery barrage started at 8 a.m. onthe 7th and at about 7-45 a.m. the battalion started moving forward to get level with the general line of the troops on both flanks.

The battalion carried out the attack in the following formation :- A Coy. on the left (under Lt.Crosbie, 2/Lt.Powell being on leave) B Coy. in the centre (under Lt.Hodgson, Captain Bowler having gone to hospital) C Coy. on the right (under Capt. Samuelson). D Coy. (under 2/Lt.Lockley, Lt.McAdam being on battle surplus) was held in reserve. Each of the front line Coys. had two platoons in the first wave and two platoons in the second wave. D Coy. attacked with its four platoons in line.

Little opposition was met with until the leading waves had crossed the line of the Guyencourt-Longavesnes road (in E 14 d & c & c E 20 a) where it ran up against very heavy m.g. fire from the direction of Saulcourt Wood (E 15 central) and also from Grébaucourt Wood (E 20 b E 21 a & b) where the attack was held up by the intensity of the fire. The right of C Coy. with the 74th Division on their right soon cleared the latter wood but their left as well as B & A Coy. and the 10th Battalion on the left were still held up by the fire from Saulcourt Wood. At the same time the enemy's artillery, which up to this had been quiet, became very active and shelled all round the area where the battalion ever held up and also Grébaucourt Wood as soon as C Coy. had entered it.

At this period HQ. which was following up by a series of bounds, leaving signalling station in rear for communication back to Bde, arrived at Hill 140 (E 20 a). The two 18 pounders attached to the battalion had not as yet turned up, but two other guns which gallopped up into the vicinity of battalion HQ. were requested to turn the guns on to the suspected position of the Mgs. Previous to this Bde.HQ. had been informed of the situation and other batteries were also turned on to the wood.

A Coy. then attacked the southern portion of Saulcourt Wood and began to push through it and B Coy. to push down the valley between the two woods also the left flank of C, the right flank of which was further forward in touch with the 74th Div. who were pushing towards Villers Faucon. (E 22 E 23).

As soon as A coy. began to make good progress through Saulcourt Wood 2/Lt. Lockley was instructed to send two platoons of D Coy. to clear the southern portion of the wood and to "mop up" behind A Coy. Seven prisoners were taken there.

The advance continued without serious opposition until it reached jsut east of Jean Copse (E 16 a & c) where it again came under m.g. fire this time from the spur running S from Capron Copse (E 17 a & b). This spur was attacked and the enemy withdrew but as soon as the line reached the crest of this spur it came under heavy m.g. fire from the direction of Epéhy and also heavy artillery fire. The three leading companies advanced rapidly down the slope under heavy enfilade m.g. fire until they reached the line of the railway embankment in E 18 c where they were under cover from fire.

By this time HQ. had been established in a trench under a small bank at E 16 d 4 9 with D coy. about 100 yds. in front.

The situation at this time (11.30 a.m. or 12 noon?) was as follows:- On the left the 12th div. had been held up some distance W of Ephy and in the rear of the 10th London. As Epehy was still held by the enemy the 10th were unable, despite several attempts, to advance further than Copron Copse 800-1000 yds. in rear of the Q.V.R., at the same time the Q.V.R in their advance down the slope towards the railway embankment had closed considerably to the right leaving a large part of the battalion front uncovered. On the right C.Coy were in touch with the 74th div. who were pushing patrols through St.Emilie. A patrol from the Q.V.R. had established itself at the Station (E 18 d 8.3).

D Coy. were therefore sent forward to the Capron Copse Line (?whether D Coy. got to the Northern or S trench of this Line) to act as a defensive flank. A Coy. were ordered to send out posts to link up with D coy. across the valley, while D & B Coys. were ordered to feel to their left. No further advance could be made to the objective during the day owing to the istuation on the left.

Late in the afternoon verbal instructions were received that the division '58th) were very anxious that the battalion should push forward during the night and occupy the trench system N & E of St.Emilie from E 18 b 1.4. to F 19 b 25.1. The 10th were to attempt to occupy the trench in E 18 a defensive flank in the Capron Copse Line. The 74th Division were also trying to push forward to the same trench system as the Q.V.R.

(My feet at the time were causing me a great deal of pain and prevented me walking any more).

I explained what was required to Captain Samuelson and instructed him to take over the 3 forward forward coys. and push forward at dusk and occupy the trench system before dawn. D Coy. were instructed to stay in the Capron Copse system.

As soon as it was dusk patrols were pushed forward from A. B. & C. Coys., and by dawn on the 8th they were all in position though very scattered owing to their numbers and the distance to be occupied. The right of C.Coy. were in touch with the 74th div. who were however some distance behind. It subsequently transpired that on the morning of the 8th the battalion was the most easterly of all British troops in France.

During the night orders were received from the Bde. that the 74th Division were taking over a bigger front and would be pushing through the battalion and that as soon as they had passed through would be withdrawn from the line and go back to Guyencourt.

In the morning a battalion of the 74th Division started to attack through us but were held up before they reached our line. The battalion was therefore unable to withdraw. During the day the battalion of the 74th div. gradually came up to our line and occupied the portion not held by us.

Shortly after the attack started information was received from Captain Peabody of the 12th London whose Coy. was in Kildare Avenue that the battn. had passed him going strong but that the Coy. of the Div. on the left, who were to assemble N of the road, had not turned up.

The attack progressed satisfactorily and by keeping well up to our barrage the battalion succeeded in taking all its objectives and after a certain amount of fighting in the trenches the garrison of the post ran off. The Coy. of the Suffolks had turned up the sunken road leading to Catelet Trench instead of one leading to Kildare Post with the result that the enemy in his flight ran into some of this Coy. and left 6 or 7 prisoners behind including an officer.

Several machine guns and a captured Lewis gun were found in position in Kildare Lane and Kildare Post and these would undoubtedly have caused the battalion considerable trouble and many casualties if the Coy. had not kept close up to our barrage thus giving the enemy no time to get these guns in action. One gun at least did get into action as the assaulting Coys. reached the trench and 2/Lt.Hart was killed. +

+ The Officer casualties in this battle were heavy

Killed.   Lt.Sedgley.   2/Lt.Hart   2/Lt.Sanctuary.

Died of wounds.   2/Lt.Lacey.

Wounded.   2/Lt.Redman. and I believe one or two more,

The gun was soon put out of action.

D Coy. who had been detailed to establish a liaison post at the cross roads at X 22 C.6 6 were unable to do so as the troops on the left had not turned up and furthermore any attempt to get to the cross roads was checked by M.G. fire.

About 5 a.m. on the 23rd the Coy. who should have attacked on the left of the Battn. turned up, having got lost on the previous night and occupied Limerick Post without opposition and a liaison post with them was established by D Coy. at X 22 c 4.3 (approx).

During the morning (?about 10 o'clock) of the 23rd a party of the enemy about 50 strong came down the sunken road running N & S through X 22 b & d unpercieved under the cover of the bank and forced an entry into Dados Lane and Dados Loop and started bombing outwards. The situation at one time became serious as the supply of bombs taken in the attack began to run short and the enemy pushed forward in both directions. Captain Peabody of the 12th Londons in Kildare Avenue organized carrying parties and sent up bombs and L.G. ammunition from his trench. At the same time supplies were sent up from Battn.HQ. at X 26 a 5.2 to Kildare Avenue whence they were carried to the front line. After considerable fighting particularly on B Coy's. front the enemy were driven back, leaving 2 wounded prisoners in our hands, and the position was re-established. During the fighting Lt. Hodgson had some hard fighting as the enemy nearly reached his Coy.HQ. 2/Lt.Lacey, who afterwards died of wounds also did stout work in driving the enemy out.

After the line had been re-established steps were taken to deal with any similar attempt that might be made under cover of darkness.

During the afternoon orders were received that the battalion and the company of Suffolks attached were to be relieved that night (Sept. 23/24th by a battalion + (?which) of the 12th Division who were taking over the front in accordance with the plan of attack for the 18th.

The relief went off without any incident, save that the relieving battalion had only half as many men as were in the section (in fact shortly afterwards information was received that the enemy had recaptured a portion of these trenches). The battalion marched to Villers Faucon where the cookers were waiting with tea and porridge and at 5 a.m. on Sept. 24th the battalion embussed and proceeded to huts and shelters in the neighbourhood of Bernafay Wood, near Montauban, where they arrived about 7 or 8 o'clock. On the journey thebusses passed through Combles and Leuze Wood schemes of heavy fighting on the part of the 1st Battn.Q.V.R. in the Somme Sept. 1916. The area thae battalion came to was the same as that occupied by the first battalion when leaving the Somme in 1916 and was close to the trenches near Carnoy occupied by the 1st Bn. from August 1915 to Jan.1916.

On the afternoon of the 24th Major-General Ramsey commanding the 58th Division and Br.-General Cobham commanding the 175th Brigade came and congratulated the battalion on the fine work they had done. The Divisional Commander reported that General Rawlinson commanding the 4th Army had rung up and congratulated the battalion on the success of their attack on the evening og Sept. 22nd.

The Battalion stayed near Burnafay Wood until the morning of Sept.26th when they marched to Dernancourt, via Montauran Mametz Fricourt and Meaulte, part of the road taken by the 1st. Bn. when they marched from the Somme on their way to Picquigny.

On the way to Dernancourt the battalion met Lt.-Col.Powell returning from hospital, on arrival at this village the battalion entrained and proceeded to Aubigny whence they marched to huts at Camblain L'Abbé.

           R.H.Lindsey Renton,
              Major.

(Received from Mr Tansey & put with
Diary, 7th July 1937. Leo)

Q.V.R. (9/London Regt).
Copy of personal notes on operations from
August 12th. 1918.

to

September 26th. 1918.

From Major W.H.Lindsay-Renton,DSO.,TD.,

-o-o-o-o-o-o-o-o-o-o-o-o-o-o-o-

Reference
France.
62nd N.E.
1/20000.

1. Notes on operations etc of Q.V.R. between August 12th and September. 26th.

After the action in Malard Wood and Tailes Wood the battalion withdrew for a night to the neighbourhood of Square J.18 and from there back on the following day to the Bois Escardonneuse on August 13th. to tents and bivouacs, while in the area training was carried out, the men washed, clothing and equipment were cleaned up

N.B.
Captain Rolls M.C., who had been in command for most of these operations was awarded the bar to the M.C.
Lieut.-Colonel Powell went on leave on August 11th.

On August 17th the Commander-in-Chief visited the 175th Bde. and saw the Bn. carry out a practice counter-attack. In the course of a conversation he laid very great stress on the following principle:- Always throw in reinforcements and reserves into places where progress is being made and not into places where you are held up. The further you progress where you are successful the more difficult it will be for the enemy to hold out in the other places

During this period 2/Lt.Powell and a platoon from D.Coy. gave a musketry demonstration to the brigade with tracer bullets with special to the fire power of a platoon where fire control and fire discipline is good. This demonstration went off very well and was very interesting.

While the battalion had been resting the division (58th) had carried out an attack on the Happy Valley which was successful at first but a counter attack drove the assaulting troops back to a line W of the Leaulte-Bray road through F.19, 25 & 26 & L.2.

In view probably of the possibility of the enemy making a further counter-attack the 175th Bde. was ordered up to the Amiens defence line (E of Tailes Wood). The Battalion went on the left of the line with its left flank on the railway at K 5 d 6.8 and its right flank on the track at K 12 b 2.7.

The Rangers (12th London) were on the right with the 10th London in reserve. Troops of the 47th Division were in front where the line had ended after the attack on Happy Valley, and also on the left.

D Coy (left) and B Coy (right) were in front in the Amiens defence system. A Coy in close support from K 5 d 1.5 to K 11 b 4.9 and C Coy in reserve in K 11 b & d. Battn.H.Q. in some old dug outs at K 17 b 2.8. At this time Captain Mayer commanded A Coy, Captain Bowler B, Lieut.Hodgson C and Lieut. McAdam D.

It is interesting to note that at this period the three battalions in the 175th Bde. were all commanded by officers of the Q.V.R. the 10th being under Major J.Nichols M.C. in the absence of Lt.-Col. Cawston, and the 12th under Major S.Sampson, M.C. in the absence of Lieut.Colonel C.Lait.

+ see map for objectives etc.
On August 23rd orders were received that the 175th Bde. would attack the light ground + E of Happy Valley. The attack was to be carried out by the Q.V.R. on the left, Rangers (12th) on the right and 10th in reserve. Troops of the 47th Division were attacking on the left and the attack would bring the line up to that held by the Australians whose left flank was in the neighbourhood of the Chalk Quarry in L 3 d.

The main difficulty of the attack was Happy Valley a deep valley about 100 yards to 300 yards wide with steep high banks on the W and E sides. This valley was known to be full of dug outs where the enemy could take refuge from our barrage. The success of the enemy's counter-attack at the previous attempt was reported to be due to a number of the enemy emerging from these dug outs and so getting the attacking troops from behind.

To deal with this one company of the 10th were attached to each of the assaulting battalions for "Mopping Up". In addition the Civil Service Rifles (15th) London of the 47th Division were detailed to follow in rear of the Bde. to mop up the valley from + N to S.

+ whether N to S or S to N?

During the afternoon of the 23rd officers went up and reconnoitred the area for assembly which was to be just behind the front line as then held. This was reported to be as shewn by the dotted line on map. The reconnaissance however showed that the line was a hundred or two yds. further west.

About 11.30 p.m. the battalion moved up to the assembly area and battalion HQ. was established at L 1 b 2.2 where also were the HQ of the 10th and 12th.

Owing to the brightness of the moon I feared that the enemy would see the troops assembling for the attack and cause considerable trouble and many casualties. In fact the enemy's machine guns were very active especially on the left in front of A Coy. who had some difficulty in getting into position and it is probable that he did see movement even if he did not put it down to an impending attack.

At 1 a.m. on the 24th the barrage came down and the attack started.

The battalion attacked in the following formation:-

A Coy (left) and D Coy. (right) in the first wave to take the actual objective laid down for the battalion, B Coy. (left) and C Coy. (right) in the second wave having as their task the digging of a support line on the reverse side of the high ground running through F 27 central. One platoon from each of these coys was attached to the leading wave to deal with any immediate mopping-up required until the arrival of the Coys. from the 10th, when they were to rejoin their Coys. The Coys. of the 10th attached to the battalion followed in rear of the 2nd wave.

Considerable opposition was met with in the Happy Valley and some stiff fighting took place. A Coy, in trying apparently, to keep touch with the 47th Div, who had edged off to the left a considerable distance, left a gap between their right and the left of D Coy. and when B Coy. came up in the second wave several machine guns were causing trouble. These were rushed and their crews killed. Captain Bowler did considerable execution in the fighting also Sergts. Ridgeley, Keats and Dunn. On the right D Coy. had a similar experience and 2/Lt. Powell caused the enemy many casualties.

After the valley had been captured the mopping-up was carried on with under difficulties owing to the night being much darker and the dugouts difficult to find (I did hear later that 100 prisoners were captured here more than 24 hours afterwards though there were a large number of troops in and moving through the valley) throughout the 24th.

During the afternoon the Battalion suffered a great loss in the death of Captain Ralls who was hit by a sniper when accompanying me to the conference in connection with the attack.

The postponed attack was ordered for 2.30 a.m. on the morning of the 25th. The objective of the attack was to pass over the Gully E of Happy Valley and capture Bronfay Farm and the trenches E of it. The attack was carried out by all three battalions of the Brigade, Q.V.R. on the left, 10th in the centre, and Rangers on the right. The Civil Service Rifles (15th London) of the 47th Division were attacking on the left and the Australians on the right.

The objective given to the Battalion was the line between Billon Copse and Bronfay Wood.

The battalion assembled for the attack on both sides of the road running N & S through F 27 b & d. The assembly was carried out undisturbed and at 2.30 a.m. the barrage came down and the attack commenced. The battalion attacked in the following formation B (left) C (right) in the front line to capture the actual objective D Coy. and A Coy (the latter under 2/Lt.Powell in the absence of Captain Mayer who was wounded on the morning of the 24th) in support to make a support line in a suitable position in the neighbourhood of Bronfay Farm.

Very little opposition was met with from the enemy but some difficulty was encountered at first in getting to the objective owing, at first, to the fact that the gully E of Happy Valley was difficult to cross having high and very steep banks also the gully having several turns in it tended to throw the troops off their direction, and then, and mainly, owing to the fact that a thick mist came down making it impossible to see more than a few yards. At first units got mixed up and were ignorant as to where they were and as to the position of troops on their flank. In a short time however they were organized and pushed forward to the objective which was occupied along the whole Brigade front.
The battalion was distributed as follows:-
B & C Coys. in the old trenches between Billon Copse and Bronfay Wood; A Coy. just in rear in the trenches immediately S.E. of Bronfay Farm & D Coy. who had started consolidating some distance back were brought up to the trenches immediately N.W. of Bronfay Farm.

Early on the morning of the 25th units of the 173rd Bde. which had been closely following up the attack and sending out patrols, went through the 175th Bde. and carried on with the attack. Considerable opposition was met with from Billon Wood.

Bronfay Farm and its neighbourhood were subjected to heavy shell fire throughout the day including gas shells but despite the bad condition of the trenches mostly shallow and wide the casualties were not many.

In the afternoon orders were received that the battalion would be relieved that night by the Post Office Rifles (8th London) of the 174th Brigade and on relief would occupy Bivouacs and huts in the gully in L 28 c & d. The night was extremely dark and rain fell heavily throughout the night so that the battalion did not get back until well into the early hours of the 26th.

The battalion had then in two night attacks advanced the line to a distance of nearly 4500 under the difficulties which arose from darkness and the nature of the ground. These were overcome by careful use of the compass and excellent work by Company Officers and N.C.O's. In the attack on the evening of 23/24th the battalion met with considerable opposition and took many prisoners and killed a number of the enemy. In the attack on the morning of the 25th the battalion attacked after a very trying 24 hours conditions which made their success creditable if only for the difficulty in keeping direction and finding their objective.

The situation when the battalion started consolidating was as follows:-

A Coy. as mentioned above had gone off to the left. B Coy. being unable to find either A Coy. or the 47th Division, who were still some distance to the left of A Coy, had two platoons in an old trench which ran through F 27 a & b forming a defensive flank facing N. The + remainder of this Coy. dug in in F 27 a in touch with C Coy. on their right, a large gap existed between C and the 12th. D Coy. had reached the road running N & S through F 27 b & d and were not in touch on either flank. The enemy still had some men in the trench and 2/Lt. Powell captured a machine gun and crew of six in the trench.

+whether mopping up platoon still with A Coy?

At dawn Bn.HQ. (as well as those of the 10th and 12th) moved forward to the Forked Tree L 2 b 65.95 in accordance with Bn. orders. In the early hours of the morning difficulty was experienced in organizing the position satisfactorily as on both flanks troops finding themselves isolated and close to enemy machine guns and snipers - who were very active throughout the day and owing to the open nature of the country and the close range made all movement dangerous and caused some casualties - began to move back. This movement was stopped and later in the morning the situation became as follows:-

The Battalion of the 47th Division on the left in response to Captain Mayers request moved down to the right. A Coy. was thus enabled to move to the right also though it was still mostly in the 47th Division area. Posts were pushed out between A & B Coys. to connect up. One company from the 10th came forward to the road and filled up the gap between D Coy - who were rather in the position where A should have been - and the 12th.

This line was held for the rest of the 24th but would - but for subsequent events - have been adjusted in accordance with original plan under cover of darkness.

During the early hours of the morning Bn.HQ. was subjected to a heavy and sustained fire from 5.9 & 8" hows. The position being near the junction of the sunken roads and a railway was an obvious mark and was in addition under observation, from high ground from the direction of Trigger Wood and Ceylon Wood to the E.   It would have been impossible, there being little or no cover, to remain there without incurring heavy casualties and Bn. HQ. was therefore (as were those of the 10th and 12th) moved to the east bank of Happy Valley. This place was also kept under continual shell fire throughout the day but some protection was afforded by the bank.

At about 1.40 p.m. on the 24th orders were received that the attack would be resumed at 4 p.m. the same day. These orders had been considerably delayed in reaching Bn.HQ. A conference was held with company commanders at B.Coy. HQ. and orders hurriedly issued. In view of the fact that the assembly had to take place in the open and under continual sniping and M.G. fire it was impossible to form up in a really suitable formation. Great difficulty was in fact experienced in assembling.

As no barrage came down at 4 p.m. as arranged, I enquired of Major Sampson commanding the 12th whether he knew what was the matter and was informed that the attack was postponed. The official orders as to the postponement only reached Bn. HQ. at 5.15 p.m.

Had the attack not been postponed it was, I think, in great danger of being a failure. The short time available, the necessity for assembling in the open by daylight with the enemy close at hand and the fact that the Bn. was not properly reorganized and could not be same under cover of darkness all militated against the success of the operation.

The battalion stayed in the gully resting until the afternoon of the 27th when orders were received to go forward and occupy the trenches between Billon Farm and Contour Wood where they remained until the following evening. This period was without any occurrence of interest.

Ref:-
France
sheet
62 c N.W.
1/20000.

On the morning of the 28th verbal orders were received that the 175th Bde. with the 1/4th Suffolks (Pioneers) attached would relieve the 173rd and 174th Bdes. that evening in the trenches E of Maricourt which had been the German front line system in 1916 before the opening of the Battle of the Somme. The Suffolks were to be on the left holding the Bois d'En Haut (A 18), Q.V.R. from their right to Support Copse with a laison post there with the 12th the next battalion, with the 10th on the extreme right.

On receipt of the above orders I proceeded with Captain Duncan (the Adjt) and reconnoitred the line. We found that the Brigades in the line had just carried out an attack and the situation was far from clear and it was exceedingly difficult to find how to take over the line.

It took a considerable time to find any Bn.H.Q., and to select the battalion which appeared to be holding the sector to be taken over.

Eventually I decided to relieve the 3rd London (173rd Bde) who appeared to be according to account to be the only battalion in the sector. Their most forward company was in the trench running N & S through A 17 d 85.00 to A 17 d 85.60.

Arrangements were made for the relief and on my return to Bn.HQ. a proportion of officers and N.C.O's were sent up to get to their trenches by daylight in order to get a good idea as to their trenches before dusk.

During the afternoon written orders for the relief were received and those showed the front line as being a good thousand yards ahead of where it had been pointed out to me. I explained this at a conference at Bde. HQ. that evening and received instructions that if the line was not held by the other Bde., I was to push forward a company before dawn and establish an outpost line there overlooking the valley running though Jigsaw Copse (B.13.d) and Battery Copse (B.20 a & c).

Just before the Bn. marched off a wire was received that the Bdes. in the line had orders from the Div. to push forward to the outpost line before relief. This had not been done when the Bn. took over.

While the relief was in progress and officer from the 2nd. London turned up and stated that a company of that battalion was in front of the 3rd London in the trench running N.W from Support Copse through A 24 a & A 18 c. Arrangements were made to alter the relief and to relieve the company. As soon as the relief was completed A Company under 2/Lt. Powell was ordered to push forward and establish an outpost line in accordance with instructions received from Bde. This was done and at dawn A Coy. was dug in along the high ground in A 18 d and A 24 b. in touch with the Suffolks in Bois d'En Haut. Touch with the 12th was not got until daylight. This was a very satisfactory piece of work on the part of A Coy. in view of the difficulties which naturally arise in pushing forward nearly 1000 yards immediately after relief with no idea as to the enemy's position and in view of the short time available for the men to get out and dig themselves in by dawn.

The rest of the battalion was distributed as follows D on the left B on the right with 3 platoons each in the trench running N.W from Support Copse with a platoon each in support in the trench running N & W through A 17 d 85.00 to A 17 d 85.60.

C Coy. in reserve in the old German front line in the vicinity of Battn.HQ. which were at A A 23 b 1.5 (approx).

No sign of the enemy could be seen at daybreak and it was believed that the enemy had withdrawn. Messages were also received that the Australians had entered Hindleg Wood (B 26 c & d) and that the division on the left was also pushing forward. The battalion received orders not to push forward until receipt of orders to do so.

Meanwhile Cavalry patrols were seen entering Maurepas from the S.E. (B 14 b). Followed shortly afterwards by Field Artillery and later heavy artillery towed by lorries.

+ 1 or 2?

In the late morning or early afternoon the Suffolks sent forward * 2 Coys. to occupy the trench running S.W. from Maupepas, and later the battalion received orders that the Suffolks were pushing forward to the trench running S.E. from Maurepas and that as soon as news was received that they had moved the rest of the Bde. would push forward. The 10th (12th?), (I am uncertain whether the 10th or 12th were on the right of the Q.V.R, but believe 12th with 10th in front) in the same trench as the Suffolks and on the right, the Q.V.R. and 12th (10th?) in the trench running S.W. from Maurepas with the Q.V.R. on the left with the brigade (and also divisional) boundaries as follows:- Northern boundary E & W line through B 14 b 0.0., sotuhern boundary E & W line through B 26 b 0.0.

News was shortly afterwards received from the Bde that the Suffolks had started moving and the battalion moved off. On arrival at the trench allotted to the battalion it was found that the Suffolks had not all gone forward and that some had not reached the trench yet. When all the Suffolks had advanced the battalion was distributed as follows A (left) D (centre) B (right) with 3 platoons each in the trench in question and one platoon each in support. C Coy. in reserve in shell holes and gun pits between the trench and the road running from S end of Maurepas through B 14 b & c and B 20 a.a.

The Battalton stayed in the situation for the night of the 29th, and in the early morning about 3 a.m. orders were received that the advance would be resumed on the 30th and that the 175th Bde. with Cavalry, artillery and R.E. attached would form the advanced guard but that the main guard would not move forward until the van guard (cavalry) had reported on the situation. [As Lieut.-Colonel Powell arrived early that morning I received orders to go back to the Transport lines near Maricourt as battle surplus and therefore I know nothing more at the period than the fact that the Bde. moved forward in the direction of Marrieres Wood and that orders were received by the battalion to carry out an attack which eventually did not come off.]

On the 31st the division was relieved by the 74th Division and on the same day the battalion came back to rest in bivouacs and shelters in Fargny Wood (A 28 b A 29 a). While in this locality training was carried out and the men bathed etc.

During the period of rest Lt.General Godley then commanding the 3rd Corps paid a visit to the Headquarters of the 175th Bde. and congratulated battalion commanders on the splendid work done by their battalions.

On Sept. 5th Lt.-Colonel Powell had an accident, owing to a bridge over a branch of the Somme giving way under his horse, and had to go to hospital.

Ref:- Map A.

On Sept. 6th the Bde. received orders to take over the line from the 47th Division. Officers were sent up to reconnoitre and at about 5 p.m. the battalion embussed and proceeding via Bouchavesnes (c 14) and Moislains (C 18) to the Nurlu-Peronne road.

This was unusually far forward for busses as the battalion HQ. of the battalion in the line was on this road and the front line was only just east of Aizecourt-Le-Bas.

On arrival at the debussing point I proceeded to Bde. HQ. and learnt that the Brigade was to carry out an attack on the following morning. The attack was to be carried out by the 10th on the left, Q.V.R. on the right, and 12th in support. The objective for the battalion was the high ground just east of St. Emilie (F 13 c F 19 a) the 10th to continue the line to the N with the 12th Division on their left, and the 74th division were also attacking on the right. The advance to be made was over 7000 yds.

The line taken over by the Battalion on the night of the 6th was on Hill 145 (D 18 & 24) E of Aizecourt-Le-Bas, where battn. HQ. spent the night in a Nissen Hut, and was about 1000 yds. in rear of the line on both flanks. The battalion was therefore ordered to advance level to the general line before the attack started.

A section of 18 pounders, a machine gun section, and 2 Stokes Trench mortars were attached to the battalion.

The attack which was carried out without an artillery barrage started at 8 a.m. on the 7th and at about 7-45 a.m. the battalion started moving forward to get level with the general line of the troops on both flanks.

The battalion carried out the attack in the following formation :- A Coy. on the left (under Lt.Crosbie, 2/Lt.Powell being on leave) B Coy. in the centre (under Lt.Hodgson, Captain Bowler having gone to hospital) C Coy. on the right (under Capt. Samuelson). D Coy. (under 2/Lt.Lockley, Lt.McAdam being on battle surplus) was held in reserve. Each of the front line Coys. had two platoons in the first wave and two platoons in the second wave. D Coy. attacked with its four platoons in line.

Little opposition was met with until the leading waves had crossed the line of the Guyencourt-Longavesnes road (in E 14 d & c & c E 20 a) where it ran up against very heavy m.g. fire from the direction of Saulcourt Wood (E 15 central) and also from Grêbaucourt Wood (E 20 b E 21 a & b) where the attack was held up by the intensity of the fire. The right of C Coy. with the 74th Division on their right soon cleared the latter wood but their left as well as B & A Coy. and the 10th Battalion on the left were still held up by the fire from Saulcourt Wood. At the same time the enemy's artillery, which up to this had been quiet, became very active and shelled all round the area where the battalion ever held up and also Grêbaucourt Wood as soon as C Coy. had entered it.

At this period HQ. which was following up by a series of bounds, leaving signalling station in rear for communication back to Bde, arrived at Hill 140 (E 20 a). The two 18 pounders attached to the battalion had not as yet turned up, but two other guns which gallopped up into the vicinity of battalion HQ. were requested to turn the guns on to the suspected position of the Mgs. Previous to this Bde.HQ. had been informed of the situation and other batteries were also turned on to the wood.

A Coy. then attacked the southern portion of Saulcourt Wood and began to push through it and B Coy. to push down the valley between the two woods also the left flank of C, the right flank of which was further forward in touch with the 74th Div. who were pushing towards Villers Faucon. (E 22 E 23).

As soon as A coy. began to make good progress through Saulcourt Wood 2/Lt. Lockley was instructed to send two platoons of D Coy. to clear the southern portion of the wood and to "mop up" behind A Coy. Seven prisoners were taken there.

The advance continued without serious opposition until it reached jsut east of Jean Copse (E 16 a & c) where it again came under m.g. fire this time from the spur running S from Capron Copse (E 17 a & b). This spur was attacked and the enemy withdrew but as soon as the line reached the crest of this spur it came under heavy m.g. fire from the direction of Epéhy and also heavy artillery fire. The three leading companies advanced rapidly down the slope under heavy enfilade m.g. fire until they reached the line of the railway embankment in E 18 c where they were under cover from fire.

By this time HQ. had been established in a trench under a small bank at E 16 d 4 9 with D coy. about 100 yds. in front.

The situation at this time (11.30 a.m. or 12 noon?) was as follows:- On the left the 12th div. had been held up some distance W of Ephy and in the rear of the 10th London. As Epehy was still held by the enemy the 10th were unable, despite several attempts, to advance further than Copron Copse 800-1000 yds. in rear of the Q.V.R., at the same time the Q.V.R in their advance down the slope towards the railway embankment had closed considerably to the right leaving a large part of the battalion front uncovered. On the right C.Coy were in touch with the 74th div. who were pushing patrols through St.Emilie. A patrol from the Q.V.R. had established itself at the Station (E 18 d 8.3).

D Coy. were therefore sent forward to the Capron Copse Line (?whether D Coy. got to the Northern or S trench of this Line) to act as a defensive flank. A Coy. were ordered to send out posts to link up with D coy. across the valley, while D & B Coys. were ordered to feel to their left. No further advance could be made to the objective during the day owing to the istuation on the left.

Late in the afternoon verbal instructions were received that the division '58th) were very anxious that the battalion should push forward during the night and occupy the trench system N & E of St.Emilie from E 18 b 1.4. to F 19 b 25.1. The 10th were to attempt to occupy the trench in E 18 a defensive flank in the Capron Copse Line. The 74th Division were also trying to push forward to the same trench system as the Q.V.R.

(My feet at the time were causing me a great deal of pain and prevented me walking any more).

I explained what was required to Captain Samuelson and instructed him to take over the 3 forward forward coys. and push forward at dusk and occupy the trench system before dawn. D Coy. were instructed to stay in the Capron Copse system.

As soon as it was dusk patrols were pushed forward from A. B. & C. Coys., and by dawn on the 8th they were all in position though very scattered owing to their numbers and the distance to be occupied. The right of C.Coy. were in touch with the 74th div. who were however some distance behind. It subsequently transpired that on the morning of the 8th the battalion was the most easterly of all British troops in France.

During the night orders were received from the Bde. that the 74th Division were taking over a bigger front and would be pushing through the battalion and that as soon as they had passed through would be withdrawn from the line and go back to Guyencourt.

In the morning a battalion of the 74th Division started to attack through us but were held up before they reached our line. The battalion was therefore unable to withdraw. During the day the battalion of the 74th div. gradually came up to our line and occupied the portion not held by us.

Late in the afternoon orders were received from the Bde. that the Battalion would withdraw at dusk. The battalion accordingly withdrew to trenches and huts on the W outskirts of Guyencourt.

On the evening of Sept. 10th while resting at Guyencourt information was received from the Bde. that the situation on the Divisional front was obscure and that the battalion must take steps for its own protection. A Coy. was therefore detailed to provide outposts round the village of Guyencourt. These outposts were withdrawn at 6 a.m.

On Sept. 11th the 175th Bde., with the 2/24th London Regt., who had recently arrived from Palestine and who had been put into the 173rd Bde, attached, received orders to take over the divisional front. The 12th London, who had been lent to the 173rd Bde. on the previous night and had been holding the trench system in W 29 & E 5 from the E & W grid line between squares W Z 3 & W 29 to the east and west grid between squares E 5 & E 11, side stepped to the left and occupied the trenches in W 29 only with a Coy. in Tottenham Post (W 30 c) the Q.V.R. took over the trenches evacuated by the 12th in E 5 and the 10th the trenches in E 12 a & b. The 2/24th were in reserve along the Sunken road in E 4 a & c.

The battalion took over the sector as follows:-
B (left) D (Centre) C (right) in the trenches in E 5 b & d with 3 platoons each in the front trench and one platoon in the support trench. A Coy. in reserve in the trench in E 5 a & c. Battn. HQ. was established in the Sunken road in E 4 c.

The tour of duty in this sector was fairly quiet on the battalion front and was quite a rest for the men after the frequent fighting and advancing.

On the morning of Sept. 12th the enemy put down a heavy barrage on the Bde. front which was intense on the front of the 12th, and shortly afterwards raided Tottenham Post and killed or captures most of the garrison. Shortly afterwards about 50 of the enemy were seen in Wood Farm just south of Tottenham Post and the artillery was put on to them. 100 rounds rapid fire from a battery was put on to this place and the enemy were not seen any more. (During this tour in the trenches 2/Lt. Adamson was killed by a shell).

Towards the end of the tour 4 platoons of the 2/24th and 4 of the Q.V.R. changed places to allow the Q.V.R. a rest and at the same time give the 2/24th an insight into warfare on the western front. This would have continued but the 2/24th were withdrawn from the Bde.

On Sept. 15th the battalion was relieved by the Post Office Rifles (8th London) of the 174th Bde., and moved back to bivouacs and tents in Ville Wood just W of the Nurlu Peronne road.

Nothing of interest occurred whilst the battalion was resting in the wood except that one night there was a gale and rainstorm of exceptional violence lasting over two hours. Numbers of tents were blown over and practically everything was soaked. It was the worse storm I have experienced for its intensity.

On Sept. 17th orders were received that an attack was to be made on Sept. 18th on Epéhy and Peziéres by the (?20th) Div. on the left the 58th Div. in the centre and the 12th Div. on the right. The general scheme was roughly that the 58th Div. were to pass forward through Peziéres and take Poplar Trench (x 26). The div. on the left and the 12th on the right were to attack at the same time and after the 58th had taken Poplar Trench the other divisions would push forward and the 12th would take over the front of the 58th which would be squeezed out. This attack met with considerable opposition both in Peziéres and Epéhy where a lot of hand to hand fighting took place but both these places were eventually carried by storm.

The 175th Bde. were in Corps reserve round Guyencourt to which place the battalion moved at about 9 a.m. on the 18th. The disposition of the battalion was as follows:- B Coy. in the Sunken road running N.W. from Guyencourt through E 3 c & E 2 d, C Coy. in the trench N of this road in E 3 c, and D Coy. in the trench S of this road in E 9 a, and A Coy. in the Sunken road in E 2 c & E 8 a.

During the day orders were received that the battalion would remain in the area for the night but that the men could be put into huts etc. B & C Coys. accordingly were distributed in huts in Guyencourt A & D Coys. remaining in their previous positions.

The battalion stayed here for the 19th and on Sept. 20th received orders to take over the front line where the situation was that the 173rd Bde had taken Poplar Trench but the division on the flank had not gone sufficiently far forward to squeeze them out.

The battalion took over the sector as follows:-
A (left) B (right) in Poplar Trench and Fir Support, East of the Sunken road in X 26 a, C (under 2/Lt.Lavington, Captain Samuelson being on leave) and D (under Lt.McAdam) in support in Fir Support, W of the sunken road in X 26 a, and Beech Avenue. Bn. HQ. was established in the railway cutting about X 25 a /.2.

On the same night orders were issued that the 10th and 12th battns. were to attack Kildare Post X 28 b and the trenches in X 28 b & X 22 d. The plan was roughly that the 10th Battn. were to attack Kildare Post and the trenches around it whilst the 12th attacking in rear were to form a defensive flank along Kildare Avenue. The Q.V.R. received orders to put Bridges over Poplar Trench to enable the 12th, who were assembling in rear of the trench, to pass over. This was done by raising duck boards from the floor of the trench, which had been the English Front Line at some time before the German offensive, and laying them across the trench.

The attack started at 5 a.m. on the 21st under an artillery barrage but was unable to achieve its object. The two battalions came under heavy M.G. fire from both Kildare Post and also Limerick Post to the N. The survivors of the 10th with the 12th ended up in Kildare Avenue.

The battalion stayed in Poplar Trench during the 21st and in the evening D Coy went forward and dug posts in the bank of the Sunken road in X 27 a. They were exposed to a great deal of shelling and M.G. fire and suffered some casualties.

At about 7 a.m. on the morning of the 22nd orders were received that the battalion must be prepared to cayyy out the same attack on receipt of orders to move. A conference with Company Commanders was held at B Coy's H.Q., and orders issued.

Later in the morning the B.G.C. 175th Bde. came up to Bn. HQ. and said that the division wanted theattack to be carried out that day as soon as an attack which was taking place on Limerick Post had succeeded. (In view of the fact that it would be necessary to move the battalion forward in small parties in order to get to a jumping off place I asked for and was granted 3 hours notice before attacking). Should the attack on Limerick Post not come off that day the battalion would have to attack at night. I pointed out that it was known that there were machine guns in Kildare Post and that the enemy were still in possession of the high ground to the N and that an attack by daylight would be in grave danger of failing and asked that it might be carried out by night. The General agreed but said that orders from higher authority were urgent. I pressed him to ask again that it should be done at night.

In view of this conversation another conference of company commanders was held and orders issued for a night attack should that be decided on.

Later in the morning I received orders to attend a conference at B.H.Q. at 2 p.m. where I was informed that permission had been obtained to carry out the attack in the night.

The general plan was as follows :- The Div. - (?which) on the left were making an attack on Limerick Post with one company attacking from the W and one Coy. from the N from the direction of Meath Post (X 21 b) which was in our hands; at the same time the Q.V.R. were to attack Kildare Post from the W while a company of the 1/4th Suffolks (Pioneers) who were to be attached to the battalion would assemble in the neighbourhood of Catelet Copse (X 28 d) which was in British hands and attack from the S. A standing barrage of about 20 minutes to half an hour was arranged to be put on Kildare Lane & Kildare Post to lift off the N position - that portion in X 22 c - 12 minutes before it lifted off the remaining portion which was further E.

The assembly area was a N & S line through the junction of Kildare Avenue and the sunken road at X 27 a 3.9. the coy. of the division on the left assembling N of the junction the Q.V.R. S of the junction.

In view of the above orders another conference of company commanders had to be held and orders issued for the attack.

During the afternoon information was received that a company of the division on the left had attempted to take Limerick Post and had been driven back, later news was received that the head of the battalion in Kildare Avenue had withdrawn some distance down the trench in a westerly direction. This vitally affected the position of the Q.V.R. as if the enemy got into this trench he could bring an enfilade fire to bear upon the battalion as it attacked towards Kildare Post. Arrangements were therefore made for the troops in Kildare Avenue to push forward again.

Information was received in the evening from Lt.Crosbie commanding A Coy. that the Coy. who had failed to take Limerick Post reported the presence of German M.G. in front of the post and that in his opinion there were also M.G's firing from in front of Kildare Post.

Arrangements were hurriedly made with the Bde. to alter the barrage to deal with these guns. The barrage was accordingly arranged to come down 300 yds. W of the line of Trenches and then to creep back at the rate of 100 yds. in 4 minutes until it reached the trench line and then carry on as before.

Late in the afternoon the Coy. of Suffolks moved off to take up its assembly position and after dark the battalion took up its assembly position. At 9.30 p.m. the barrage came down and the attack started.

The battalion attacked as follows:- B Coy. on the left under Lt.Hodgson to capture Kildare Lane from the sunken road at X 22.c 3.1 to trench junction in X 28 a 70.95 then to work up Dados Lane and Dados Loop as far as its junction with Sprint Trench at X 22 d 45.00. On capturing this a block was to be established in Stone Trench; A Coy. on the right under Lt.Crosbie to capture remainder of Kildare Lane also Kildare Post and then work up Holts Trench and Sprint Trench and join up with B Coy. on completion of this to establish a block in Catelet Trench.

In support D Coy. on the left under Lt.McAdam to take over and mop up the portion of Kildare Lane captured by B Coy. and to hold this and a portion of Dados Lane, on the right C Coy. to act similarly with the remainder of Kildare Lane and Kildare Post and take over the portion of Holts Trench. The Coy. of Suffolks after assisting in the capture of Kildare Post were to hold the line of the sunken road running from X 28 central to Kildare Post.

Shortly after the attack started information was received from Captain Peabody of the 12th London whose Coy. was in Kildare Avenue that the battn. had passed him going strong but that the Coy. of the Div. on the left, who were to assemble N of the road, had not turned up.

The attack progressed satisfactorily and by keeping well up to our barrage the battalion succeeded in taking all its objectives and after a certain amount of fighting in the trenches the garrison of the post ran off. The Coy. of the Suffolks had turned up the sunken road leading to Catelet Trench instead of one leading to Kildare Post with the result that the enemy in his flight ran into some of this Coy. and left 6 or 7 prisoners behind including an officer.

Several machine guns and a captured Lewis gun were found in position in Kildare Lane and Kildare Post and these would undoubtedly have caused the battalion considerable trouble and many casualties if the Coy. had not kept close up to our barrage thus giving the enemy no time to get these guns in action. One gun at least did get into action as the assaulting Coys. reached the trench and 2/Lt.Hart was killed. +

+ The Officer casualties in this battle were heavy

Killed.   Lt.Sedgley.   2/Lt.Hart   2/Lt.Sanctuary.

Died of wounds.   2/Lt.Lacey.

Wounded.   2/Lt.Redman. and I believe one or two more,

The gun was soon put out of action.

D Coy. who had been detailed to establish a liaison post at the cross roads at X 22 C.6 6 were unable to do so as the troops on the left had not turned up and furthermore any attempt to get to the cross roads was checked by M.G. fire.

About 5 a.m. on the 23rd the Coy. who should have attacked on the left of the Battn. turned up, having got lost on the previous night and occupied Limerick Post without opposition and a liaison post with them was established by D Coy. at X 22 c 4.3 (approx).

During the morning (?about 10 o'clock) of the 23rd a party of the enemy about 50 strong came down the sunken road running N & S through X 22 b & d unpercieved under the cover of the bank and forced an entry into Dados Lane and Dados Loop and started bombing outwards. The situation at one time became serious as the supply of bombs taken in the attack began to run short and the enemy pushed forward in both directions. Captain Peabody of the 12th Londons in Kildare Avenue organized carrying parties and sent up bombs and L.G. ammunition from his trench. At the same time supplies were sent up from Battn.HQ. at X 26 a 5.2 to Kildare Avenue whence they were carried to the front line. After considerable fighting particularly on B Coy's. front the enemy were driven back, leaving 2 wounded prisoners in our hands, and the position was re-established. During the fighting Lt. Hodgson had some hard fighting as the enemy nearly reached his Coy.HQ. 2/Lt.Lacey, who afterwards died of wounds also did stout work in driving the enemy out.

After the line had been re-established steps were taken to deal with any similar attempt that might be made under cover of darkness.

During the afternoon orders were received that the battalion and the company of Suffolks attached were to be relieved that night (Sept. 23/24th by a battalion + (?which) of the 12th Division who were taking over the front in accordance with the plan of attack for the 18th.

The relief went off without any incident, save that the relieving battalion had only half as many men as were in the section (in fact shortly afterwards information was received that the enemy had recaptured a portion of these trenches). The battalion marched to Villers Faucon where the cookers were waiting with tea and porridge and at 5 a.m. on Sept. 24th the battalion embussed and proceeded to huts and shelters in the neighbourhood of Bernafay Wood, near Montauban, where they arrived about 7 or 8 o'clock. On the journey the busses passed through Combles and Leuze Wood schemes of heavy fighting on the part of the 1st Battn. Q.V.R. in the Somme Sept. 1916. The area thae battalion came to was the same as that occupied by the first battalion when leaving the Somme in 1916 and was close to the trenches near Carnoy occupied by the 1st Bn. from August 1915 to Jan. 1916.

On the afternoon of the 24th Major-General Ramsey commanding the 58th Division and Br.-General Cobham commanding the 175th Brigade came and congratulated the battalion on the fine work they had done. The Divisional Commander reported that General Rawlinson commanding the 4th Army had rung up and congratulated the battalion on the success of their attack on the evening og Sept. 22nd.

The Battalion stayed near Burnafay Wood until the morning of Sept. 26th when they marched to Dernancourt, via Montauran Mametz Fricourt and Meaulte, part of the road taken by the 1st. Bn. when they marched from the Somme on their way to Picquigny.

On the way to Dernancourt the battalion met Lt.-Col. Powell returning from hospital, on arrival at this village the battalion entrained and proceeded to Aubigny whence they marched to huts at Camblain L'Abbé.

R.H. Lindsey Renton,
Major.

Army Form C. 2118.

WAR DIARY
or
INTELLIGENCE SUMMARY

9th Bn. London Regt. Queen Victoria's Rifles

(Erase heading not required)

Place	Date	Hour	Summary of Events and Information	Remarks and references to Appendices
	1918 Oct. 1		Battalion in the line N. of LENS. Bn. HdQrs. at M.14.c.45.50. Quiet day.	
	2		Quiet day.	
	3		A/B Coys. pushed forward through LENS and established posts along road running from N.21.a.8.5 to N.15.a.4.5. 175th Bde. on the Bn. left. 11th across Bn. front joining up with 20th Divn. on Bn. right in front of LENS, centering 175th Bde. dvk. The forward Companies were withdrawn. Forwards M.18.c., M.24.a & M.14.d.	
	4		Quiet days.	
	5			
	6		Battalion moved back to huts and at MARRUEFFLES FARM. R.26.v.3.6.	
	7		Morning – discovery re-equipment. Afternoon, firing on range.	
	8		Firing on range.	
	9		175th Bn. relieved 174th Bn. in Right Brond Sectr. Bn. less 1 company, relieved 8th Lond. Regt. F.O.R. in reserve. Remaining company attached to 12th Lond. Regt. Remain in the line. Bn. H.Q. at M.6.a.15.30. Quiet day.	
	10		Quiet day. Slight shelling of reserve position at night.	
	11		Quiet day. Slight shelling in vicinity of Bn. H.Q. at night.	
	12		Quiet day.	
	13		Battalion moved forward to support position at HARNES turns billets in area O.9.R. (u.v.a. Moved Bn. H.Q. at O.9.Z.6.4. E.A. active at 21.00 hrs. dropping bombs in vicinity of billets.	
	14		Quiet day.	

Power. Major.
Commdg. Queen Victoria's Rifles.

WAR DIARY

9th Bn. London Regt. *Queen Victoria's Rifles*

INTELLIGENCE SUMMARY

Army Form C. 2118.

Place	Date	Hour	Summary of Events and Information	Remarks and references to Appendices
	1918 Oct 15		Battalion relieved 6th Bn. London Regt. in front line. Bn. H.Q. at O.18.c.85.95.	
	16		During early morning A Coy. pushed 2 platoons across canal + held remainder of "A" and C + D Coys. worked canal on improvised bridges. D Coy. pushed forward through BOIS d'HARPONDIEU + cleaned the wood with C Coy. on their right. A Coy. pushed one patrol E toward P.10.d. Cnt. P.10.d.5.8 and FOSSE 8, and obtained liaison with Royal Berks (12th Divn) on their right. B Coy. moved forward in support along canal. Stick in P.2.a + c. Bn. H.Q. moved forward to JERUSALEM as P.1.a.65.	
	17		In conjunction with Bde. on flanks, Bn. continued the advance meeting with little opposition + by dusk reached line of railway running N + S through Q.4.410. Coys. on flanks pushed forward patrols + gained touch with 9th London on left + Berks on right. At 2:00 hrs Bn. relieved by 12th London + returned to billets at MIDRENEAUX.	
	18		Advance continued. Bn. forming part of main body. At night Bn. took up reserve position + Bn. dispositon in hutments in Bepre at L.31.c. Bn. H.Q. at K.36.c.9.3.	
	19		Advance continued. Bn. forming part of main body. Bn. billeted for night at LE BASHAMEAU in support.	
	20		Advance continued. Bn. plus 1 section R.E., 1 section M.G., 1 section M.G. formed Advance Guard, passing through NOMAIN at 08.00 A.M. 1 Platoon B Coy. plus 1 cyclist acting Scouts in advance of Advance Guard. No resistance by enemy. At 14.00 hrs Bn. on line of front I.1.a.00 I.14.c.7.7. Bn. H.Q. at I.Y.a.4.3.	
	21		Advance continued. Bn. formed part of main body. Bn. halted in RUMEGIES from 11.00 to 14.30 hrs. PONT 121100 farms been destroyed by enemy of obstruction removed. Resistance slightest enemy.	

[signature] Major
Commdg. Queen Victoria's Rifles

WAR DIARY

9th Bn London Regt — Queen Victoria's Rifle

INTELLIGENCE SUMMARY

Army Form C. 2118.

Place	Date	Hour	Summary of Events and Information	Remarks and references to Appendices
	1918 Oct. 21		Artillery very active. At night Bn in reserve in billets at I.4.d. Bn. H.Q. at I.4.d.8.9. Enemy shelled RONCY systematically during the night.	
	22		Battalion in reserve at I.4.d. RONCY shelled by enemy during the night 22nd/23rd with H.E. & gas causing 20 casualties.	
	23		Billets shelled & Bn. moved to 301S de RONCY during the day — new Bn. H.Q. at which remained at I.4.d.8.9. Bn. relieves 12th London in the Right Sub-Sector. 1 Company in outpost line, 2 companies in support & 1 company in Reserve. Bn Hd at I.11.a.6.0. Scattered shelling on the Bn. area. Patrols during whole of the night formed enemy alert. Posts established at J.7 central & T.4.a.9.8.	
	24		Harassing fire & explosives noticed behind enemy's lines. Patrols pushed forward, meeting with little resistance & at 04.00hrs line of posts was established along railway from T.2.A.85.35 & T.9.d.3.8. Liaison established with 24th Londons on left & with 25th Am. on right. Outpost line reinforced with 2 platoons. Any patrols found bridges at T.3.C.4.0 impassable & enemy entrenched. During night of 24/25ths foot bridge put over canal at T.3.C.4.0 & T.3.C.8.8. Patrols found enemy alert.	
	25 26		MAULDE heavily shelled at intervals during this day also bridge at T.3.C.4.0. Bdr relieved by 14th Inf. Bde & Bn withdrew to billets at RUMEGIES. Bn H.Q. at I.14.a.4.0. Bn. in Divisional Reserve.	
	27		A day devoted to re-equipping, bathing &c.	
	28 29 30 31		Battalion training including firing on range	

Powell Major
Commdg. Queen Victoria's Rifles

Confidential

War Diary

of

9th Battⁿ London Regiment
(Queen Victoria's Rifles)

From 1st November 1918 to 30th November 1918

Army Form C. 2118.

WAR DIARY
or
INTELLIGENCE SUMMARY.

9th LONDON REGT. QUEEN VICTORIA'S RIFLES.

(Erase heading not required.)

Instructions regarding War Diaries and Intelligence Summaries are contained in F.S. Regs., Part II. and the Staff Manual respectively. Title pages will be prepared in manuscript.

Place	Date	Hour	Summary of Events and Information	Remarks and references to Appendices
QUMEGIES	Nov 1st		Battn in rest billets - Raining	Sheet 44
	2nd		do	
	3rd		do	
	4th		do	
	5th		C.O. & Coy Commds reconnoitred forward area	
	6th		do	
	7th		do	
	8th		Battn practiced crossing moat on rafts	
	9th		Warning order at 10 hrs that the enemy had retired on our Bde front & prepared to move that day. The 175th Inf Bde moved forward. 7/10th Battn moved into Illies in MAULDE. The 12th Battn in LE QUESNOY arriving at 18 hours. Battn H.Q. at 52 a 4.0. The Bde moved forward, the Q.V.Rs forming advance guard plus 1 section 18pdrs 10e 4.5 hows 1 section M.G. a platoon of Corps Cyclists. Passing through the outpost line (held by 174th Inf Bde) at 10 hours. A.B.C. Coys advanced via FLINES, KEGIS, ROUVIGNON, LES QUATRE CHEMINS to WIERS. D Coy via FLINES, KEGIS, 47 central, K8a. 4.4, K8c 5.5. to WIERS. Thence all Coys to PERUWELZ. No opposition was encountered throughout the day & outpost line to that night Ran on line approx F15 c 6.0 - F23 c 6.0 A. & D Coys in outpost line. B & C Coys in outpost in F 21 d. Battn H.Q F27d 3.6. The troops were enthusiastically received by the civilian population who were filling in mine craters & making roads through on villages, over rivers etc to allow us to pass on	

9th BATTN LONDON REGT (QUEEN VICTORIA'S RIFLES)

Army Form C. 2118.

WAR DIARY
of
9th London Regt Queen Victorias Rifle

INTELLIGENCE SUMMARY.

(Erase heading not required.)

Place	Date	Hour	Summary of Events and Information	Remarks and references to Appendices
	Nov 11th		The Bde continued the advance. The 12th Battn forming advance guard. 9/10th & QVRs Main Body. The main body passed starting point F27d 33 at 8 hours. Proceeded F21d 5.3, Ba BOITERIE, BASACLES, QUEVAUCAMPS, STAMBRUGES thence 2/10th Battn to NEUFMAISON the QVRs to ECACHARIES where they remained in billets for the night. Battn H.Q. at B14 b 8 0.	Sheet 44t & 45
ECACHARIES	Nov 11	10.	The 175th Bde remained in same position. Information received that at 11 hrs hostilities would cease. All units to remain in present positions. BUGLERS sounded "stand fast" "Cease fire" in the Square at 11 hrs. Battn Thanksgiving service at 11.30 hours.	
STAMBRUGES	13th		2/10th Battn relieved RANGERS in outpost line. QVRs & RANGERS the H.Q. moved into billets at STAMBRUGES. Battn HQ at H & 55.50. Bde Thanksgiving service attended by QVRs RANGERS, KTMB & Bde HQ at 10.30 hrs.	
	14th		Battn in billets. Draining during morning	
	15th		" " " " " Church Parade	
	16th		" " " " " Draining during morning	
	17th		" " " " " " "	
	18th		" " " " " " "	
	19th		" " " " " " "	
	20th		" " " " " " "	
	21st		" " " " " " "	
	22nd		" " " " " " "	

R.J. [signature]

Commdg 9th Battn. LONDON REGT
(QUEEN VICTORIA'S RIFLES)

WAR DIARY
or
INTELLIGENCE SUMMARY

Army Form C. 2118.

9th LONDON REGT — QUEEN VICTORIA'S RIFLES

Place	Date	Hour	Summary of Events and Information	Remarks and references to Appendices
QUMEGIES	Nov 1st		Battn in rest billets - Training	Sheet 44
	2nd		"	
	3rd		do	
	4th		do	
	5th		do - C.O. & Coy Commdrs reconnoitred forward area	
	6th		do	
	7th		do - Battn practice crossing moat on rafts	
	8th		"	
			Warning order at 10 hrs that the enemy had retired on our Bn front & to prepare to move that day. The 175th Inf Bde moved forward. The 2/4 R. Berks 7/10 Battn moved into billets in MAULDE. The 12th Battn in LE QUESNOY arriving at 18 hours. Battn H.Q at J 3 d 4 0.	
	9th		The Bde moves forward. The 2/4 R.Bs forming advance guard plus 1 section 1sdn 1ac. H.S. horses 1 section M.G.s, a platoon of Corps Cyclists, passing through the outpost line (held by 174th Bde) at 10 hours. A,B,C Coys advanced via FLINES, KEGIS, ROUILLON, LES QUATRE CHEMINS to WIERS. D Coy via FLINES, KEGIS, K7 central, K6a 4.4, K8c 5.5 to WIERS. Thence all Coys to PERUWELZ. No opposition was encountered throughout the day. Outpost line for that night was on line approx F15 c 09 - F23 c 60 AND Coys in outpost line. B & C Coys in outpost in F 21d. Battn H Q F 27 d 3.6. The troops were enthusiastically received by the civilian population who were falling in with cakes & making rough bridges over river etc to allow us to pass on	R.H.Husey Lt Col Comdg 9th Battn LONDON REGT (QUEEN VICTORIA'S RIFLES)

Army Form C. 2118.

WAR DIARY
9th London Regt Queen Victorias Rifle
INTELLIGENCE SUMMARY

(Erase heading not required.)

Instructions regarding War Diaries and Intelligence Summaries are contained in F. S. Regs., Part II. and the Staff Manual respectively. Title pages will be prepared in manuscript.

Place	Date	Hour	Summary of Events and Information	Remarks and references to Appendices
	Nov 16th		The Bde continued the advance. The 12th batt. forming advance guard 2/10 & QVRs main body. The main body passed starting point F.27.d.3.3. at 8 hours proceeded F.21.d.5.3. La Boiterie, BASACLES, QUEVAUCAMPS, STAMBRUGES thence 2/10 batt. to NEUFMAISON the QVRs to ECACHARIES where they remained in billets for the night. Battn H.Q at B.14.b.8.0.	Sheet 44 " 45
ECACHARIES	Nov 11th		The 175th Bde remained in same position.	
	12th	10.	Information received that at 11 hrs hostilities would cease. All units to remain in present position." BUGLERS Sounded "Cease fire" in the Square at 11hrs. Battn Thanksgiving service at 11.30 hours	
STAMBRUGES	13th		2/10th battn relieved RANGERS in outpost line. QVRs & RANGERS Bde H.Q. move into billets at STAMBRUGES. Battn H.Q at H.13.55.50. Bde thanksgiving service attended by QVRs RANGERS, LTMB & Bde H.Q. at 10.30 hrs. Battn in billets.	
	14th		" " Training during morning	
	15th		" " " " "	
	16th		" " " " "	
	17th		" " Church Parade	
	18th		" " Training during morning	
	19th		" " " " "	
	20th		" " " " "	
	21st		" " " " "	
	22nd		" " " " "	
	23rd		" " " " "	

R J Andrew Major
Commd 9th Battn London Regt
(Queen Victoria's Rifles)

Army Form C. 2118.

WAR DIARY
or
INTELLIGENCE SUMMARY

9th London Regt. Queen Victoria's Rifles.

(Erase heading not required.)

Instructions regarding War Diaries and Intelligence Summaries are contained in F. S. Regs., Part II. and the Staff Manual respectively. Title pages will be prepared in manuscript.

Place	Date	Hour	Summary of Events and Information	Remarks and references to Appendices
STANBRIDGE	23rd		Platoon Drill. Manoeuvring. Morning	Sheet 45.
	24th		Church Parade.	
	25th		Platoon Drill. Training during morning. Elementary Educational Classes started	
	26th		" " " " " Classes	
	27th		" " " " "	
	28th		" " " " "	
	29th		" " " " " Rehearsal of Div. Inspection by	
	30th		" Army Commander to be held on Dec 2nd	

R.J. Lauzen-Rendor
Major.
Commanding Queen Victoria's Rifles.

Confidential

War Diary

— of —

9th Battn. London Regt. (Queen Victoria's Rifles)

Period 1st December to 31st December 1915

Army Form C. 2118.

WAR DIARY
9th London Rgt. Queen Victorias Rifles.
or
INTELLIGENCE SUMMARY
(Erase heading not required.)

Place	Date	Hour	Summary of Events and Information	Remarks and references to Appendices
STAMBRUGES	Dec 1.		175th Inf Bde in billets in STAMBRUGES.	4.S.
	2.		58th Divn reviewed by the First Army Commander (Sir Henry Horne) on ground	
			Abad at 11 hours.	
	3		Battn training education classes etc.	
	4		" " " "	
	5		The King accompanied by the Prince of Wales Prince Albert & the Army Commander etc	
			visited STAMBRUGES. The party walked through the village talking to the troops en route	
	6		Battn training educational classes recreation etc	
	7		" " " " "	
	8		" " " " "	
	9		" " " " "	
	10		" " " " "	
	11		" " " " "	
	12		" " " " "	
	13		" " " " "	
	14		" " " " "	

Lieut Col.
Commdg 9th Battn. LONDON REGT.
(QUEEN VICTORIA'S RIFLES.)

Army Form C. 2118.

WAR DIARY
or
INTELLIGENCE SUMMARY.

9th London Regt. Queen Victoria Rifles

(Erase heading not required.)

Instructions regarding War Diaries and Intelligence Summaries are contained in F. S. Regs., Part II. and the Staff Manual respectively. Title pages will be prepared in manuscript.

Place	Date	Hour	Summary of Events and Information	Remarks and references to Appendices
STAMBRUGES	15		Platoon training educational classes recreation etc	45
	16		" " " " "	
	17		" " " " "	
	18		" " " " "	
	19		" " " " "	
	20		175th Inf Bde vacated its billets in STAMBRUGES and marched to fresh billets in LEUZE (Sheet 37)	Sheet 37
LEUZE	21		Platoon cleaning billets etc at disposal of Coy Comdr	
	22		" " " " "	
	23		" " " " "	
	24		" " " " "	
	25		Christmas day. Church parade.	
	26		Coy at disposal of Coy Commdr	
	27		" " " " "	
	28		" " " " "	
	29		Church Parade	

[signature] Lieut Col.
Commdg

Army Form C. 2118.

9th London Regt. "Queen Victoria's Rifles".

WAR DIARY
or
INTELLIGENCE SUMMARY.
(Erase heading not required.)

Place	Date	Hour	Summary of Events and Information	Remarks and references to Appendices
LEUZE.	30		Battalion training, educational classes, recreations.	
			175th Bde held a torchlight	
	31.		tattoo on the Grand Place at 21.30 hours: 40 men from each Battn took part.	

[signature] Lieut. Col.
Commdg. 9th Battn. LONDON REGT.
(QUEEN VICTORIA'S RIFLES.)

Confidential

War Diary
— of —
9th Battn. London Regiment
(Queen Victoria's Rifles)

Period from 1st January 1919 to 31st January 1919

Army Form C. 2118.

WAR DIARY or INTELLIGENCE SUMMARY.

9th London Bat. Queen Victoria's Rifles.

(Erase heading not required.)

Instructions regarding War Diaries and Intelligence Summaries are contained in F. S. Regs., Part II. and the Staff Manual respectively. Title pages will be prepared in manuscript.

Place	Date	Hour	Summary of Events and Information	Remarks and references to Appendices
LEUZE	1919 JAN 1		175 O.R. who starved in billets in LEUZE. Coys at disposal of Coy Comdrs for training. Education Classes under Battn arrangements	Sheet 37.
	2		" " " "	"
	3		" " " "	"
	4		" " " "	"
	5	11.15	Church Parade	"
	6		A & B Coy Baths C & D Coys at disposal of O.C. Coys. Education Classes	"
	7		C & D Coys " A & B " " "	"
	8		Battn Route march. Education Classes	"
	9		" "	"
	10		Coys at disposal of O.C. Coys. Education Classes.	"
	11		Battn Parade. Pay. Interior Economy. Education Classes.	"
	12	9.45	Church Parade.	"
	13		Coys at disposal of O.C. Coys. Education Classes	"
	14		" "	"
	15		" "	"

R.A. Wisemen Radn Major.
Commanding 9th London Rgt.

Army Form C. 2118.

WAR DIARY
or
INTELLIGENCE SUMMARY.

5th London Bat. London Regt. (London Rifle Brigade)

(Erase heading not required.)

Instructions regarding War Diaries and Intelligence Summaries are contained in F. S. Regs., Part II. and the Staff Manual respectively. Title pages will be prepared in manuscript.

Place	Date	Hour	Summary of Events and Information	Remarks and references to Appendices
LEUZE	JAN 16		Battn. Route March. Education Classes. D. Coy. Baths.	Appx 134.
	17.		Coys. at disposal of O.C. Coys. Education Classes. Lecture to party by Commanding Officer.	
	18.		Battn. Parade. Pay. Interior Economy. 3 O.R's departed for demobilization	
	19.	11.15	Church Parade.	
	20.		Coys. at disposal of O.C. Coys. Education Classes.	
	21.		" " " "	
	22.		Battn. Inspection by Brig. Gen. Cobham CMG DSO	
	23.		Battn. Route March. The Coys. Commdr. (Sir Arthur Holland KCB DSO MVO) inspected Rooms Dining Rooms etc. visited a performance of the Battn. Billets. Recreation Party.	
			of the Battn. Concert Party.	
	24.		Coys. at disposal of O.C. Coys. Educational Classes.	
	25.		Mon. R.H. Lindsey Renton D.S.O. assumed command of the Battn. during the absence of Lt Col E.H. Ferguson on leave.	
			Coys. at disposal of O.C. Coys. Educational Classes. 10 O.R's & W.O.R departed for demobilization.	
	26.	9.45	Church Parade. Billet inspection by Commanding Officer.	R.S. Lindsey Renton Major Commanding 5th London Regt.

Army Form C. 2118.

WAR DIARY
9th London Regt. Queen Victoria's Rifles.
INTELLIGENCE SUMMARY.
(Erase heading not required.)

Place	Date	Hour	Summary of Events and Information	Remarks and references to Appendices
LEUZE	JAN 27		Coys. at disposal of O.C. Coys - Education of Classes.	Sheet 37.
	28		" " " " " "	
	29		" " " " " "	10 Officers + 4 O.R. departed for Demobilization
	30		" " " " " "	
	31		Batts. Pay + Interior Economy + Educational Classes	

R.J. Hudson-Gordon Major
Commanding 9th Batn. London Regt.

Army Form C. 2118.

WAR DIARY
or
INTELLIGENCE SUMMARY.

9th London Rgt. Queen Victoria Rifles

(Erase heading not required.)

Instructions regarding War Diaries and Intelligence Summaries are contained in F.S. Regs., Part II. and the Staff Manual respectively. Title pages will be prepared in manuscript.

Place	Date	Hour	Summary of Events and Information	Remarks and references to Appendices
LEUZE	1919 Feb 1.		Coys at disposal of O.C. Coys for general cleaning up. Educational classes. Draft for Rhine left	
	2.	16.30	Church Parade. C.O. inspected billets after parade.	
	3.		Coys at disposal of O.C. Coys. Baths. Educational Classes.	
	4.		" " " " " Route March "	
	5.		Baths Route March " " "	
	6.		Coys at disposal of O.C. Coys " " " Draft left to be entrained.	
	7.		" " " " " Educational Classes. Draft left by train	
	8.		" " " " Payr Interior Economy Educational Classes.	
	9.	10.30	Church Parade " " Educational classes	
	10.		Coys at disposal of O.C. Coys " " Baths. Educational Classes	
	11.		Coys at disposal of O.C. Coys " " " " "	
	12.		" " " " " " " " Draft left for demobilisation	
	13.		" " " " " " " " A.D.M.S. inspects & Sanitary arrangements	
	14.		" " " " " " " " Draft left for demobilisation	
	15.		" " " " Payr Interior Economy " Draft left for Rhine	

M.W. Bell Thomas Lt. Col.
Commanding 9. London Rgt.

WAR DIARY
or
INTELLIGENCE SUMMARY.

9th London Regt Queen Victoria Rifles

Army Form C. 2118.

Place	Date	Hour	Summary of Events and Information	Remarks and references to Appendices
LEUZE	Feb. 16	10.30	Church Parade. Draft left for demobilisation	
	17		Coy at disposal of O.C. Coy. Educational Classes. Baths.	
	18		Reorganization of billets etc. Commanding inspects the battn during the morning	
	19		Coy at disposal of O.C. Coy. Baths. Draft left for demobilisation	
	20		All ranks in the battn eligible for demobilisation posted to the 12th battn. The battn on duties. Large drafts of reinforcements arrived for other battns in the divn (2½%/24 & No. 12)	
	21		The battn reorganises into four Coys. H.Q. Coy	
	22		Coy at disposal of O.C. Coy. Pay. Lewis Gunnery	
	23	16.30	Church Parade	
	24	9.15	Commanding Officer's parade. Also lecture at 11.30 hours.	
	25	9.15	" Baths. for B.D. & H.Q. Coy	
	26	9.15	" " for B. Coy	
	27		Coy at disposal of O.C. Coy. The Divisional Commander inspected battn during the morning. Battn preparing for move	
	28th		Battn entrained at LEUZE at 14 hours for DÜREN (Germany)	

Lt. Col.
Commanding 9th London Regt

Army Form C. 2118.

WAR DIARY
or
INTELLIGENCE SUMMARY.
(Erase heading not required.)

Instructions regarding War Diaries and Intelligence Summaries are contained in F. S. Regs., Part II. and the Staff Manual respectively. Title pages will be prepared in manuscript.

Place	Date	Hour	Summary of Events and Information	Remarks and references to Appendices
LEUZE	1-2-19		BATTALION AT LEUZE Inspection of Companies followed by Batn Ceremonial parade	
	2nd		ditto Church Parade, Battn adopted Brigade Roles	
	3rd		ditto Practice rehearsal for Presentation of Colours.	
	4th		ditto Ceremonial Practice Drill	
	5th		ditto Ceremonial Practice Drill	
	6th		ditto Parade for Lecture on Army of Occupation etc	
	7th		ditto Ceremonial Practice	
	8th		ditto Companies at Disposal of O.C. Companies	

Army Form C. 2118.

WAR DIARY
or
INTELLIGENCE SUMMARY.
(Erase heading not required.)

Place	Date	Hour	Summary of Events and Information	Remarks and references to Appendices
LEUZE	9-2-19		Battalion at LEUZE. Reconstruction of Battn. A Coy for Demobilization. B.D Coys for Army of Occupation. Church Parade	
	10th		Battn. proceeded to PERUWELZ for rehearsal of presentation of Colours and billeted at BOUSSE COURSE	
	11th		Battn. presented with Colours by 1st Corps Commander Lieut-Gen Sir Arthur Holland KCB DSO MVO at PERUWELZ	
	12th		Employed at disposal of OC Companies.	
	13th		D Coy Alert Route March. A.D.M.S. inspection of Battn. Area.	
	14th		Employed at disposal of OC Companies	
	15th		Employed at disposal of OC Companies, Brigade NCOs Dance	
	16th		Church Parade	

www.ingramcontent.com/pod-product-compliance
Lightning Source LLC
Chambersburg PA
CBHW081440160426
43193CB00013B/2340